STOPS ALONG
THE
MANX ELECTRIC RAILWAY

OR

'WHAT WE DID ON OUR HOLIDAYS'

GEORGE HOBBS

Loaghtan Books
Caardee
Dreemskerry Hill
Maughold
Isle of Man
IM7 1BE

Published by Loaghtan Books

First published: July 2014

Typesetting and origination by:
Loaghtan Books

Printed and bound by:
Geerings Print

Website: www.loaghtanbooks.com

ISBN: 978 1 908060 09 9

For my long-suffering wife,
with love

(Is this the right thing to say, Dear?)

Front cover: Car 2 and trailer 59 southbound at Ballagorry. 28 July 2013

Rear cover: Winter saloon 22 heading for Laxey at Skinscoe. 5 October 2013

Title page: Stop flag at Skinscoe. 9 May 2002

CONTENTS

Contents   3

Introduction   3

Stops along the line   5-139

Appendix - passenger facilities at MER halts   140

Selected Bibliography   140

INTRODUCTION

The Manx Electric Railway (MER) connects the Isle of Man's capital, Douglas, with Ramsey, the island's second largest town, almost eighteen route miles away to the north up the east coast. The first part of the line, to Groudle Glen, opened on 7 September 1893 with extensions to Laxey (28 July 1894), Ballure (2 August 1898) and finally Ramsey (24 July 1899). The line was laid to the same gauge as the Isle of Man Railway (IMR), 3'-0", and is double track throughout. Electrified at 500 Volts DC with overhead line, current collection was initially by Hopkinson bow collectors which were superseded after a few years by the more familiar trolley pole and wheel.

The line was one of the earliest electric lines in the British Isles, the promoters realising that they had a choice between extensive civil engineering works to reduce the gradients sufficiently to permit steam working or using electric power on a more affordable but hillier line. The line was originally promoted by the Douglas Bay Estate Ltd., with the formation in 1893 of the Douglas & Laxey Coast Electric Tramway which took over the transport aspects. Then on 30 April 1894 the tramway undertaking was renamed the Isle of Man Tramways and Electric Power Co. (IoMT&EP), and, not only generated its own power but also provided the first public electricity supply on the island.

The collapse of Dumbell's Bank in February 1900 caused considerable difficulties for the Isle of Man and, like many island companies, the IoMT&EP found itself facing severe financial problems. Eventually the tramway passed to new owners, becoming the Manx Electric Railway on 18 August 1902 and retaining this name today.

The MER was profitable in its early years. Its route to Ramsey was not ony more direct than that of the Manx Northern Railway route through St John's and Kirk Michael, its service was more frequent and faster and so captured the bulk of the passenger traffic. The absence of competition on most of the MER route, including the important mining village of Laxey, also contributed to the company's financial returns.

As a major holiday destination, the Isle of Man had many seasonal visitors and the MER carried large numbers of passengers, especially to tourist attractions such as the glens at Garwick, Dhoon and Ballaglass, which it owned. Not surprisingly the First World War curtailed the holiday trade and the reduced passenger numbers affected the MER's financial stability. Although the holiday trade recovered after the war, the advent of competing motor bus services, the depression of the 1930s, and the Second World War had a serious effect on the MER's viability. The growth of private motoring, coupled with the increasing costs of maintaining the by then ageing infrastructure and cars, meant that the MER was almost bankrupt by the mid-1950s.

Mounting losses made the MER board unwilling to continue in business and it proposed to close the line. Fortunately negotiations took place with the Manx government which resulted in nationalization of the MER in 1957. Under the new ownership the backlog of maintenance was addressed but profitability was not restored. As a cost-cutting exercise the MER service was curtailed in 1975 with the closure of the line between Laxey and Ramsey and the total suspension of winter services. The postal service, whereby lineside boxes were emptied by MER conductors, was transferred to road vans at the same time.

The closure between Laxey and Ramsey was extremely unpopular on the island and, following a hard-fought campaign, the line re-opened in June 1977. The full length of the MER has continued in operation ever since, apart from a few months in 2008 when urgent engineering work between Laxey and Ramsey caused a temporary closure. At the time of writing there is no scheduled winter service and the MER effectively operates as a tourist line during the season. Extended timetables apply during the TT race fortnight when a more intensive service caters for the massive influx of visitors. Special railway enthusiast events are also organized, often in conjunction with the steam railway, when more intensive operations bring more and different cars out of the depots.

Unlike the majority of British tramway systems, trailer cars have always been used on the MER and there are almost as many trailers as power cars. The total passenger fleet acquired comprised thirty-two motor cars (seventeen saloon and fifteen open) and thirty trailers (three saloon and twenty-seven open). A fleet of freight stock, including post vans and open wagons and one electric freight locomotive, was also purchased. In 1930 a major fire destroyed the Laxey car shed together with four motor and seven trailer cars. Although the motor cars were not replaced, three new trailers were purchased in 1931 to what was then an out-of-date design. In 1990 a fire at the Derby Castle car shed destroyed the body of power car 22. This was rebuilt as a replica on the original underframe and re-entered service in 1992.

It is very unusual for a tram company neither to have chosen to replace its aging rolling stock, nor to have increased its fleet in over one hundred years. The last planned fleet increase was in 1906 and the MER continues to operate with its original rolling stock; the three 1931 replacement trailers and the replica 22 are the only passenger vehicles which are less than one hundred years old. Not all the surviving trams are serviceable and the current peak service level is maintained by about half the total fleet. The remaining vehicles are stored out of use.

In order to provide engineering support a diesel-electric locomotive, which can provide motive power when the electricity supply is switched off, was constructed in 2007-8. Although the diesel engine is modern the rest of the locomotive re-uses much old equipment. Its bright yellow livery contrasts with the traditional colour schemes of the passenger vehicles.

The MER follows the rugged east coast of the Isle of Man with many steep inclines and sharp curves. Starting from near sea level at the Derby Castle terminus at the north end of Douglas Bay, the main intermediate station is reached at Laxey after seven miles and approximately thirty minutes running time. This is the interchange point for the Snaefell Mountain Railway which climbs the island's highest mountain, Snaefell, at 2,034 ft.

Between Laxey and Ramsey the route's most spectacular section is near the summit at Bulgham, 588 ft above sea level, where the track runs along a ledge cut into the cliffs with a sheer drop to the rocks below. The northern section of line is largely rural and the typical running time is forty-five minutes for the eleven miles between Laxey and Ramsey.

Between Douglas and Ramsey there are more than sixty recognised stops. The major manned stations with booking offices are Douglas, Laxey and Ramsey. The remaining stops vary between the obvious intermediate points with waiting shelters and nameboards to the minor wayside halts where the only evidence may be a sign strapped to the upper part of a traction pole. In some cases where the pole has been replaced recently even this may be missing. To alight at any stop inform the conductor when boarding the car, to board give a clear signal to the motorman.

This book illustrates all the current stops along the line from Douglas to Ramsey, with a variety of trams, trailers, shelters and other items of interest at each location. The number of pictures at each stop reflects the author's judgement on the likely interest, and photographic merit of the available material. Accordingly some minor halts may appear to be over-represented. Wherever possible the derivation of each stop name is given with reference to the history of the area and other information which the author hopes may be interesting.

The photographs are the product of many happy hours spent travelling on the MER, as well as enjoying the idyllic Manx countryside and observing tramcars in the setting they were designed to serve. All the pictures were taken between 1996 and 2014 and few of them have appeared in print before.

For further details about the MER the reader is advised to consult the selected bibliography where sources far more authoritative than the current author are listed.

In the words of a long-departed conductor, noted as a raconteur: 'All aboard for a magic carpet ride to Ramsey'!

Not *the MER!* *'MER car 17'* *is an approximately two-thirds replica operating at Seaton Tramways, Devon, England.* *7 October 2010*

For many people their first view of the Manx Electric Railway is as they approach the Derby Castle (Douglas) terminus along the promenade. The workhorses of the electric line are the four winter saloons (numbers 19-22), constructed in 1899 and still going strong into the twenty-first century. Below winter saloon 20 arrives at the terminus and,

according to the 'Next Car Leaves' clock board, is due to form the 4:10 pm northbound service. Car 20 is carrying a special vinyl poster on its dash commemorating that 2013 is the one hundred and twentieth anniversary of the MER. There is a different vinyl on the Ramsey end of the car.

In common with many railway stations the Douglas facility of the MER is not quite as near the town centre as most travellers would like. When the railway was proposed, permission was granted by Tynwald in the Howstrake Act of March 1892 to construct a single or double railway line adjacent to any road which was over 36 ft wide on the Howstrake Estate stretching north of Douglas. Use of electricty as motive power was in its infancy and a bold choice for the new consortium. Permission was also granted to reclaim land at Port-e-Vada by filling in the creek to provide space for the depot and generating station. Port-e-Vada appears to be a corruption of *Port-e-Vaatey* or possibly *Port-y-Artay* ('port of the small boat'), *baatey* being Manx for a boat about the size of a large rowing boat. 22 September 2013

The Isle of Man Steam Railway celebrated 125 years of operation in 1998 and this was met with celebrations and events across the island's railway network. MER tunnel car 9, delivered in 1894, was fitted with illuminations and suitable commemorative displays as part of the festivities of the MER centenary in 1993 and these were adapted for the steam railway's 125 year celebration.

Car 9 is seen here at Derby Castle alongside the rustic MER booking office which dates from the opening of the line. Intending passengers should, in railway style, buy their tickets at the booking offices of the major stations (Douglas, Laxey and Ramsey) where possible. Conductors sell on-board tickets for passengers joining the cars at intermediate points. The rustic nature of the hut is created by affixing split logs to the structure and is a feature of other structures along the line. 5 May 1999

Derby Castle was constructed by Major Samuel Pollack in 1836 on land he had purchased from the estate of the Duke of Atholl six years earlier. The Major also built Strathallan Lodge next door, where he and his family lived. Strathallan Lodge is now the Terminus Tavern which is conveniently, and logically, situated next to the MER and Douglas Horse Tram termini. The inn sign of the Terminus Tavern features MER car 1, one of the three original power cars from 1893.

At the time of the construction of the railway the foreshore was owned by Douglas Town Commissioners, but the area inland is in Onchan, so the MER terminus is only just within the town limits. The obvious extension of the MER along the promenade to the Victoria Pier has never taken place, and passengers are still faced with a change to bus, horse tram or walking the two miles to arrive at the town centre or the ferry terminal. 6 May 2008

From inn sign to the real thing; car 1 is seen at Derby Castle in the historic livery of the Douglas & Laxey Coast Electric Tramway and still at work despite it being more than one hundred years since she first set off along the line to Groudle in 1893. The main difference in appearance is the substitution of the trolley pole for the Hopkinson bow collectors originally used on this pioneering line.

Bow collectors are still used on the Snaefell Mountain Railway to ensure that continuous contact with the overhead allows no break in the power for climbing the steep incline. Meanwhile the art of current collection has moved on and nowadays the usual means of providing power to a tramcar is by pantograph. The MER, however, still relies on the traditional trolley pole and wheel. Quite a lot of skill is required to place a highly sprung and therefore heavy pole onto the overhead with minimal arcing. 3 May 1999

Derby Castle is the interchange point between the Douglas Corporation horse cars and the electric cars of the MER. In the background can be seen the red-painted shutters of the horse car depot.

Car 7 is resplendent in its new blue and white livery following its major rebuild in 2009-10. At the same time the seating was rearranged from the original longitudinal pattern to a transverse (2+1) layout. Cars 5 and 7 have transverse seating while cars 6 and 9 retain longitudinal benches. 12 May 2012

This is the interior of tunnel car 7 as it was before its refit. The car is standing at Derby Castle before working a northbound service. At the time car 7 was unique among the longitudinally seated tunnel cars as it was fitted with upholstered seat cushions – cars 6 and 9 retaining wooden benches.

Subsequently car 7 spent several years with the engineering department before being rebuilt with transverse (upholstered) seating and re-entering public service in 2011.

Outside the right-hand windows is Leyland National bus number 26, which was in use as a waiting room for the tramway. Prominent lettering above the windows advertises the MER's presence to prospective passengers on the promenade. 11 May 1998

The Summerland leisure complex is just visible behind tunnel car 6 which is arriving at Derby Castle from Ramsey. It is a replacement structure as the original burned down on 2 August 1973 in one of the worst fires in peacetime Britain. Fifty people died. Here car 6 is in front of the Aquadrome, part of Summerland's successor, which has now also been demolished (see, for example, page 5). The original arrangement of the cab windows of the tunnel cars is seen here, with twin droplights. During the 1980s the twin windows were replaced on all four of the surviving cars of the 4-9 series by single windscreens which allowed greater visibility for the driver than the original arrangement. In 1991, car 6 had the original twin window arrangement reinstated following accident damage, but has now again adopted the single end-window style. 5 May 1996

The MER has particular appeal, as the rolling stock is practically all original and dates back to the Victorian or Edwardian eras. Winter saloon 22 (below) is one exception. Whilst stabled in Douglas car shed on the evening of 30 September 1990, fire broke out in the resistances and destroyed the original 1899 bodywork. Minor damage was also sustained by cars 17 and 19 which were stabled nearby.

The bodywork of car 22 had gone, but losing one of its four winter saloons would have had unacceptable effects on the MER service. Accordingly a new body was built by McArd Contractors of Port Erin, and car 22 was able to re-enter service on 22 May 1992. The rebuilt car is not quite a replica as it incorporates electric bells and other changes, but it does reflect most of the winter saloons' original Victorian features.

For a couple of years car 22, alone on the MER, ran in the livery pictured. It was based on the then current Isle of Man Transport bus livery, and car 22 sported it to promote the integrated nature of the Island's transport services. The car has since reverted to a more traditional colour scheme. 5 May 2001

A trailer sandwich! The last operating day of 2013 finds an unusual threesome of cars at Derby Castle (left). The Douglas-end controller of car 6 (in the foreground) developed a fault on the southbound run, when the parallel notches became out of order. The car proceeded at reduced power on the series notches with sluggish climbs up from Laxey and Groudle and a consequently delayed arrival at Douglas.

Help had been summoned from the car sheds and winter saloon 21 was despatched to take over the next northbound duty. Meanwhile car 6, sporting a vinyl dash panel commemorating 120 years of the MER, will run forward and return to the shed for attention. Trailer 46, now coupled to car 21, will then be shunted into the departure road and the combination of car 21 and trailer 46 will head back to Ramsey following a slightly late start. 3 November 2013

From time to time the MER cars appear in historic liveries. Here car 19 is in the livery of the Douglas, Laxey and Ramsey Electric Tramway, a progression on the title carried by car 1 (see page 6), which was the form used prior to the Ramsey extension opening. Car 19 has arrived with trailer 47 and is drawing onto the landward line in order to allow the trailer to be rolled down to the departure line.

From Derby Castle the traction poles are numbered in sequence, so pole 1 naturally represents the start of the line. Occasionally extra poles have been inserted to smooth out curves in the overhead, and at these points suffixes are added to the previous pole number, e.g. '156A'. Excepting the section beside the road at Ramsey, the traction poles are generally a single line centrally placed between the tracks, with bracket supports for each wire, but on some of the sharper curves more complex netting is used to give a smoother line and minimise instances of de-poling.

Behind looms the concrete Aquadrome, another building which has disappeared from the Douglas seafront. At the time of writing, as can be seen in the picture above, this plot is still vacant. 11 May 2000

The supply of spare parts for historic vehicles is a problem; the manufacturers are either no longer in business or are not willing to produce obsolete components economically for a much-diminished market. In the mid 1990s, therefore, the MER purchased car 360 from Lisbon in Portugal and brought her to the Isle of Man as a source of spare components for use on the Manx fleet. About four years after arriving, and following removal of the trucks, the body of the Lisbon tram was placed at Derby Castle and, for a time, became a passenger shelter. Installation at Derby Castle took place on 4 May 2000 and here the superstructure is resplendent in its Lisbon advertising livery. 9 May 2000

What a difference a day makes! By the time of the last car to Ramsey on the next evening, the lower bodywork had changed from advertising red-orange to the deep maroon shown here.

The car was originally delivered to Lisbon in 1908, so post-dates most of the MER native fleet, as indeed does the Lisbon tramway which opened in August 1901. The difference in the body styling between the Portugese and Manx trams is very noticeable, although would have been less marked had the Lisbon car retained its clerestory roof which was removed during a rebuild in 1959-61. 10 May 2000

The complete repaint of Lisbon 360 provided the car body with a mainly maroon paint scheme with cream cant rail band, as shown in this photograph taken the following year. The 'Wait Here For Trams' inscription is, sadly, not to the usual high standards of the MER sign-writing team, but on a wet and windy day the car body provided a useful respite from the elements. The body also provided a more tramway orientated ambiance compared with the previous facility, the redundant Leyland National bus number 26 observed through the windows of car 7 on page 7.

The Portuguese tram body has long since been replaced by a green painted steel and glass bus-type shelter (what a pity!) across the end of the tracks, which can also be used by those waiting for northbound buses on the promenade.

The body of the ex-Lisbon tram was rescued from a scrapyard in Ballasalla near Ronaldsway airport during 2013, and, having been refurbished, now resides in a private garden in that area. 5 May 2001

A relatively unusual sighting at Derby Castle is open motor car 32 with lightweight trailer 51. Having arrived from Ramsey these cars have unloaded and are about to shunt back to the depot.

Cars 32 and 33 were the last pair of motor cars bought by the MER in 1906 and have the most powerful motors in the fleet. The set pictured here had been chartered for a photographic special by Nick Meskell of *Trams* magazine and has returned to base at the end of the shoot. Trailer 51 has been restored to original condition; as delivered in 1893 it was one of the first six trailer cars, and has been known to appear as number 13. 6 May 2004

Another unusual trailer to find at Derby Castle is the lightweight 36. It had been brought from Laxey car shed by tunnel car 6 the previous day (see page 50) when the shed was being evacuated and the stored cars brought to Douglas for off-line storage in the former Isle of Man Road Services Homefield bus garage. Later in the day 1894-built trailer 36 was collected by the road hauliers and taken away from

the rails it had inhabited for so long. Looking rather dishevelled the car was still capable of being towed and there is always the possibility that it may be restored to service in due course. 8 May 2002

At the start of each season the MER cars need to be woken from their hibernation and brought back into serviceable state. One of the problems is that cold weather and a humid environment can lead to condensation in the motors. A build-up of water can cause insulation failure in electric motors so that they become temperamental or to fail to start. Early in the season it is not unusual, therefore, for cars to be taken on a round trip to Laxey for a 'drying out' run where the warmth of the motors dries out any moisture (see also page 41). These runs take place first thing in the morning, before the normal service starts, so that any problems will not interfere with fare-paying passengers. Cars on such runs are accompanied by fitters so that any remedial action can be taken on the spot rather than calling for assistance. Here we see paddlebox motor 26 after it has returned from such a drying-out run. 7 May 2004

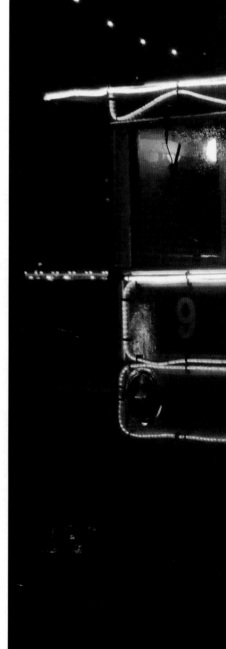

In the summer the MER and the Snaefell Mountain Railway organize evening dining events at the hotel on Snaefell summit. Leaving Douglas in the early evening, diners transfer at Laxey to the mountain line.

After dinner and descent from the mountain, the return to Douglas offers a relatively rare opportunity to travel on the MER after dark. At 10:00 pm on a dark (and rainy) evening we see illuminated car 9 at Derby Castle. Car 9 has brought saloon trailer 57 from Laxey (with the trailer interior lights connected to the motor car's supply) and is about to return to Laxey without the trailer to collect the second group of diners.

The friendly welcome exuded by a warm and illuminated tram on a dark and rainy night is not easily forgotten. However familiar one is with the MER, travelling in the dark is a new experience and the absence of visible landmarks once beyond the street lights at Far End (see page 21) on King Edward Road is particularly noticeable. On this night the tram de-poled near Eskadale (see page 29) but the conductor successfully restored power despite having to work in almost total darkness. For the Snaefell diners a late night car also operates to Ramsey in the peak season. 18 May 2012

When the Manx Electric Railway was nationalized by the Manx Government in 1957 it decided that a new corporate livery was appropriate. This was a light green and white scheme which is carried by car 16 in its historic livery re-enactment as shown here. Trailer 60 is also painted in this scheme and so, when coupled together, a vintage late-1950s scene can be recreated.

Crossbench motor car 16 dates from 1898 and is currently the only member of the batch 14-18 which is in serviceable condition. The modern image green livery was never applied to the whole fleet, was often said to be disliked, and reverted to the traditional style before too long. 14 May 2005

Tunnel car 6 poses at Derby Castle. From the condition of the car it is clear that it has had a repaint during the previous winter and it positively gleams in the spring sushine. Meanwhile in the background car 19 in its historic livery awaits departure time on the next northbound service. The parked Douglas Corporation horse cars are extolling the virtues of the MER and hopefully have been ferrying passengers along the nearly two-mile-long promenade. With the buses stopping next to the tram terminus, Derby Castle is a genuine, if unusual, public transport interchange. 10 May 2001

Car 22 and trailer 41 stand at Derby Castle having arrived from Ramsey and are about to perform the normal shunt manoeuvre to reverse the formation. A classic example of Victorian tramway vehicles? Well, that is the appearance, but, as noted on page 8, car 22 was rebodied in 1992 following fire damage.

Trailer 41 is one of three new trailers purchased from English Electric in 1931 to replace some of the trailers lost in the major fire at the Laxey car shed in 1930. Trailers 40, 41 and 44 took the numbers of three of those lost in the fire. So the combination of car 22 and trailer 41 represents the MER at its most modern rather than the Victorian image pictured by most passengers. This might shatter some illusions, but it is important to realise that the MER is a living railway and keeping the fleet active is part of the job. 5 May 2008

The first stop after leaving Douglas is Port Jack at pole 16, the steepness of the climb and the sharp curve mean that cars will normally only stop on the descent into Douglas and not when climbing the hill – passengers take note!

Port Jack was originally called *Purt Cooyn* ('narrow creek'). The recluse Jack Kermeen had a rough camp here and the area duly acquired his name. The stream is now in a culvert beneath the line.

The Douglas Bay Hotel stood for many years to the north of the creek and was the first customer to be supplied with electricity by the tramway for its 250 electric lights. Skandia House now occupies the hotel's site; the MER climbs round the south and east sides of the property.

The shops at Port Jack date from around 1912. Winter Saloon 21 with trailer 47 climbs past them on its way north. 18 May 2010

What many passengers who ride on the MER fail to realise is that behind these shops is the entrance to Port Jack Glen; the entrance archway is just visible from trams descending around Onchan Head. The glen is landscaped with paths and a culverted stream winding through it which later crosses beneath the tram tracks.

The close proximity to the tramway of the row of shops is very clear. Note the MER sign which requests pedestrians to use the walkways provided rather than risk the trip and slip hazards of the rails and sleepers directly outside the shop doorways. 13 May 2012

ONCHAN HEAD

Onchan Head (pole 33) forms the northern protection of Douglas Bay and for many years was home to an informal fair ground. The Howstrake Estate Company leased the site to William Cubbin and Harold Mylcreest in 1908 and they constructed a fun fair with roller coaster, roller skating and live entertainment. The land was sold to Mr Cubbin in 1913 and proved to be a popular venue with over 20,000 visitors per day in the holiday seasons of the 1920s. Later known as White City Amusement Park the traffic justified a manned ticket office. White City closed in 1985 and nowadays the area has become part of the Douglas and Onchan urban area and is given over to housing.

When business no longer required lavish facilities such as the ticket office, a name board (with individual signwriting) and waiting bench was thought to suffice. Ideal if it's a sunny day. 2 May 1999

In 1999, shortly after the previous picture was taken, the facilities were modernized. The steel and glass bus shelter now serves not only the MER but also the bus service which runs along King Edward Road. Stop flags for both modes of transport are duly displayed, as well as timetables for both services. Such shelters have been provided at several locations along the line and, whilst undoubtedly providing weather protection on less-than-perfect days, the modernity is in stark contrast to the previous facilities. Unfortunately no prospective passengers today. 18 May 2010

Unusually there are two cars on the northbound line. Car 9 has its trolley pole tied down and car 22 has come up behind. Car 9 is being used for a tram-driving experience course and the instructor has brought the car up to Onchan Head. Here the participants are given their first hands-on experience of the controls, but with the power disconnected for safety reasons. Onchan Head offers an almost flat and straight section of track with which to gain a feel for how a tram under power will respond.

Whilst the would-be motormen are inducted, car 22 has come up from behind and will need to wait a while. From here car 9 will proceed to Laxey where the second trainee will transfer to the south end and return the car to Douglas under the watchful eye of the instructor. 15 May 1998

Winter saloon 20, with trailer 46, heads towards Ramsey passing the stop at Onchan Head with the now thirteen-year old shelter visible to the right of the picture. Note that the bus stop flag is no longer present; the 'flag' is now on the window. The number 13 bus still serves King Edward Road but, at the time of writing, there are only two per day.

Behind the tram Douglas Bay is visible and already the climb up from near sea level is apparent. 13 May 2012 *(Sara Goodwins)*

This stop, at pole 46, takes its name from one of the former names of the dining establishment situated above the line; the restaurant is the large white building on the top of the embankment on the tram's right. Built in 1924 for Mrs Harriet Hart, the first eatery on this site was called the Café Royale, courtesy of a competition in the Manx Press, and for some years the stop had the same name. The Hart family ran the café until it was commandeered during the war to act as a convalescent home.

After the war the diner changed hands and became a B&B, but by the 1960s it was known as 'The Sizzler Café Royale' and specialized in grills. More changes of owner and name followed. 'Julian's', 'Boncompte', 'Woodford's', 'The Top Table', 'Churchill's' and then a Chinese restaurant 'The Water Margin'. At the time of writing it is still a Chinese restaurant but now trades under the name 'Majestic'. This raises the possibility of confusion with the next stop.

Having just boarded the service car on its way north to Ramsey, the photographer is on the rear row of seats of trailer 48 hauled by winter saloon 19. Heading south are car 6 with trailer 43, photographed through the rear window of 48. 11 May 2007

MAJESTIC

Shortly after Churchill's is Majestic at pole 51. Named after the hotel which stood across the road, the building started life as View Park Mansion. Built in 1893 by Mackay Hugh Baillie Scott, the 'Arts and Crafts' architect who lived for twelve years on the Isle of Man, View Park Mansion was enlarged in 1922 and converted into the Hotel Majestic. When it opened it advertised as having ninety five bedrooms, although two years later this had mysteriously risen to 150, and by 1937 it claimed to have 200 bedrooms, sixty two of them with their own bath. In 1935 the owners also purchased Fort Anne Hotel on Douglas Head. During the Second World War the Majestic was used as a military hospital, sending some of its patients down King Edward Road to the Café Royale to convalesce (see above).

With the decline in visitors the grounds were taken over for residential building and the hotel closed in 1987. The decaying remains were finally demolished and the Majestic Apartments began to grace the site from 2004. The MER continues past, and the hotel is still remembered in the name of the stop.

It is now late in the season and there are few holidaymakers, so winter saloon 22 will suffice for the expected passengers with no trailer needed today. 5 October 2013

BRAESIDE

Having been successful with View Park Mansion (see Majestic), in 1896-7 Baillie Scott designed and built the pair of semi-detached villas Leafield and Braeside, collectively known as Parkview Villas. The front finish of the houses includes a line of twelve roundels, formed from pebbles, and painted black. Similar roundels appeared on the mansion, and could still be seen on the hotel it became. Above the door of Leafield is written 'Welcome ever smiles, but farewell goes out sighing', a quotation from Shakespears's *Troilus and Cressida* (act III, scene iii), while over the door of Braeside is a quotation from Alexander Pope's poetic working of Homer's *Odyssey* (book XV, line 84) ' Welcome the coming, speed the parting guest'. Opposite Braeside, and on the other side of the road, winter saloon 20 and trailer 46 coast downhill towards Douglas. 13 May 2012 *(Sara Goodwins)*

A few seconds later the photographer has captured the car set from behind. Maybe the weather is not as warm as might be expected in May as there are no takers for seats on the trailer today. The Braeside halt is at pole 59. 13 May 2012

Car 20, now with trailer 40 in tow, climbs towards the Braeside stop – the stop is just behind the photographer – on its way north. The arrival of the MER in 1893 clearly increased the attraction of living along the new line with views over Douglas Bay to the south. Recognising a business opportunity the house builders duly followed the tramway builders. The prospect of an easy journey to Douglas by electric and horse tram could not have escaped prospective purchasers of the new houses. By 1898 Braeside was occupied, although Leafield was not, which may explain why the stop took the name of the former only.

The tramway also directly influenced the naming of the road which runs parallel to it. It was the visit in August 1902 by King Edward VII and Queen Alexandra, and their journey by tramcar next to the road, which is believed to have been responsible for its patriotic name. 16 September 2011

In the UK the regulation of tramways required that the electrical supply be broken into half-mile sections. Although UK regulations do not apply to the Isle of Man, similar principles are followed. Here we see the Braeside stop traction pole with a splendid array of feeder wires for each of the electrical sections on either side of the pole.

The overhead is fed at 550 volts DC and there is no electrical continuity between the sections, so, in order to eliminate arcing and consequent damage to the overhead and trolley wheels, drivers must shut power off when running across the break in the circuit. Inside the car, passengers will be concious of a momentary flicker of the saloon lights as the insulated section is crossed. Naturally the breaks in the circuit are arranged so that they do not interfere with the efficient operation of the tramway and steep hills and sharp corners are generally avoided. 13 May 2012

Far End (pole 66) takes its name from the large house on the opposite side of King Edward Road from the tramway. This is the furthest point along the road before the tramway turns the corner round the hill, so probably this was the last house to have a view of Douglas. When the tramway was built the house stood alone in large grounds but now, at the time of writing, a gated community of four five-bedroomed dwellings is being developed on the plot.

Tunnel car 9 with trailer 43 powers up the hill with a northbound service and is about to round the corner and leave the urban area behind. Beyond this point the tramway skirts the King Edward Bay Golf Course, although the tramway and road are cut into the cliff here so the links are not apparent from the tramcars. 13 May 2012 *(Sara Goodwins)*

Winter saloon 20 and trailer 40 have stopped to allow passengers to alight from the first service car from Ramsey in the morning. The driver has released the brakes and notched up enough to get the car rolling, after which the car set will coast most of the mile or so to Douglas; passengers often don't realise how little power the tramcars need to draw in some sections. In this view the abbreviation on the car's rocker panel incorporates three full stops. Frequently, when the abbreviated form is used by signwriters, the final full stop is omitted. 16 September 2011

Shortly after the previous photograph was taken, recently rebuilt car 7, now with transverse 2+1 seating having replaced the original longitudinal bench seating, heads north with trailer 48. The trailer has also been refurbished and is in matching blue and white livery. Interestingly the motor car is labelled 'Douglas & Laxey Electric Tramway', matching the historic livery dating from before the Ramsey extension opened, whilst the trailer bears the later title of 'Manx Electric Railway'. Squeezing the legend born by the car into the available space on the trailer would be a challenge to any signwriter. There is a good load onboard this morning departure from Douglas. 16 September 2011

One of the advantages of riding on an open trailer (or motor) is that there is always the possibility of being able to grab shots unimpeded by the windows of the tram itself. Luck is still needed not to have a close up of a traction pole, but this was a lucky day. Turning the corner on a Douglas bound car the photographer found open motor 27 at the Howstrake stop with one of the tower wagons and the poles and wires gang attending to a local problem.

At times like this, some nifty manoeuvring was sometimes necessary to keep the engineering cars out of the way of the service cars. Well-timed excursions to the nearest crossover were often necessary to shunt out of the way and back again once the service car had cleared. At this time car 27 was a regular performer with the engineering team. 9 May 2000

The Howstrake camp stop (pole 88) is situated at the summit of the line between Douglas and Groudle Glen. The camp was established in 1907 on the site of the old Cunningham Camp, the latter having moved to Douglas to a site next to Little Switzerland. Howstrake was advertised as a city under canvas for clean-living young men and was very popular in the early part of the twentieth century. It was claimed that the main dining room was the largest room on the island devoted to eating.

The concrete shelter on the opposite side of the road from the tramway was built and maintained by the Taylor family who owned and ran Howstrake Camp. Contra-intuitively the entrance to the camp – which was on the coast – was inland through the gateway at the side of the tram tracks. Campers would walk over the rise and down through a tunnel beneath the road. Although now blocked, the entrance to the tunnel can still be seen a few yards towards Groudle where the walls on either side of the road appear to be the parapets of a bridge.

It is always satisfying to capture more than one car in a photograph. Here winter saloon 19 with trailer 42 heads downhill towards Douglas, whilst sister car 22 climbs to the summit with an unidentified, but similar, trailer. 8 May 2012

In time the tents of Howstrake camp were replaced by chalet-type huts which presumably offered superior accommodation. The huts were commandeered at the start of the Second World War to house the junior arm of the Royal Marines School of Music. Despite the cramped and chilly conditions (quite reasonably the chalets were not designed for use in the winter) bandsmen remember Howstrake with great fondness, although they do say that they became very tired of a diet made up almost exclusively of Manx kippers!

In later life one instructor at Howstrake, Bandmaster 'Nutty' Duncan, became Director of Music for the Fiji police band. Island life obviously appealed, but the later position must have had some contrasts with the Isle of Man.

The camp closed in 1973 and various schemes were proposed for the site, including building new chalets and the erection of a Butlin's-style holiday experience. In 1980 fire destroyed most of the main rooms, fed by the furniture and mattresses stored within, and only the foundations of a few of the chalets now remain.

Passing the scene of faded glory on the opposite side of the road is winter saloon 21, running single motor downhill towards Douglas. 5 May 2002

A planning application by Whitgift Homes in 1994 to build 200 houses and flats with a sixty-bedroom hotel on what they considered a brownfield site was not approved by the authorities. The site remains derelict with little more than the concrete bases of the chalets to show what was once there.

The derivation of name Howstrake has a number of possibilities. It is generally taken to be from the Norse *hǫfuð* ('head') or *haugr* ('mound') with the addition of *troða* ('walk') and means 'track over the headland'. The name originally applied to the packhorse road between Onchan and Groudle, now called Groudle Old Road (see next stop), which lies on the other side of the King Edward Bay Golf Club from the tramway.

In this view car 9 is heading towards Douglas and has just restarted having paused opposite the now dilapidated shelter, which has been fenced off in recent years. Trailer 43 is in tow. 13 May 2005

The Groudle Old Road stop, sometimes known as Groudle Village or Groudle Lane, is situated between the summit at Howstrake and the major stop at Groudle Glen. The old road crosses the line at pole 107 and descends to Groudle Village. Work began on building the cottages in the new village in 1973, but was delayed by an arson attack in August; the first cottages were ready for occupation by the following March. In April 1975 the Onchan Village Commissioners, which had purchased Groudle Glen in July 1967, sold part of it, including the land on which the holiday cottages stood, to Harbour and Glen Investments Ltd., owned by Mr Dennis Jeavons, which had developed the holiday village.

The cottages near the beach still provide holiday accommodation in the summer, whilst those further up the glen are now occupied all year round. The car park near the holiday cottages was once the site of a water-powered corn mill built in the nineteenth century.

Above the holiday village, the large detached house is known as Settler's Hollow and was once occupied by Mr Jeavons. Here tunnel car 6, with 120-year celebration vinyls on the dash, has restarted from the Groudle Old Road stop. Having deposited a passenger for the village, it is coasting down to Groudle Glen. 5 October 2013

From Groudle Glen to Howstrake is a steady climb and here we see winter saloon 22 heading past the modern steel and glass waiting shelter. As Groudle village post-dates the rustic hut era presumably the provision of a shelter was not deemed necessary here in the early days of the railway. Groudle Old Road is very narrow and is therefore one way from Onchan – hence the multiple 'No Entry' signs. 5 October 2013

Winter saloon 20 with trailer 47 is departing for Douglas and faces the steady climb up to Howstrake.

Groudle Glen is noted for the narrow gauge railway which was installed in 1896 to take visitors from near the entrance to the Glen – on the other side of the road from the tram in this view – to a clifftop viewpoint where a small zoo including sea lions and a polar bear could be seen. Understandably but perhaps unimaginatively the line's two small engines were accordingly named *Sea Lion* and *Polar Bear*. With the decline in tourist traffic the railway fell into disrepair, but has now been restored to operation by a dedicated band of volunteers working hard since 1982. Trains run on Sundays throughout the summer with additional services on Bank Holidays and Wednesdays in the peak months. The line is narrow gauge (2'-0") and provides a pleasant three-quarters of a mile run to the visitor centre and café at Sea Lion Rocks.

The original *Sea Lion* locomotive has been rebuilt and is still at work. *Polar Bear* is at the Amberley Chalk Pit Museum in Sussex. Other locomotives now share *Sea Lion's* load. 19 May 2010

As can be seen in the picture at the foot of the page, parked in the corner of the Groudle Glen waiting shelter is this traction pole finial. A heavy item, but designed to keep the rain out of the traction pole and so inhibit rust formation. Consequently they were practical as well as decorative additions. 19 May 2010

At the Laxey end of the building, just creeping into the right of the shot below, is this plaque, unveiled by the island's Governor General, Sir Laurence Jones, on 7 September 1993, to commemorate one hundred years to the day since the first car arrived from Douglas. Hopefully there are many more anniversaries to come. 5 October 2013

The buildings at Groudle Glen (pole 117) are impressive and capacious, if atypical. This was the original terminus of the line opening on 7 September 1893. Although now unmanned, the ticket office survives at the Douglas end of the building and is a reminder of busier days. The concrete GROUDLE on the grass bank leaves no doubt as to the location and was installed on the stop's hundredth birthday in 1993, as was the low stone wall and paving. In the peak summer season an evening shuttle operates between Douglas and Groudle Glen, often using illuminated car 9, on two or three evenings per week. 19 May 2010

There seems to be almost a full load on board original 1893 car 1 with attached lightweight trailer 60. Behind the tram is visible a large building with a balcony which was once a hotel designed by Baillie Scott. Originally it had timber-framed stabling for three to four horses. The building was completed in 1893, at a cost of around £1,500, although the verandah was added the following year. It was owned by Richard Maltby Broadbent, the entrepreneur who developed Groudle Glen.

Having been a pub for many years, when the photograph was taken the building housed a restaurant called La Casa. At the time of writing the restaurant has been closed for some years, so the nearest refreshment available is at the Groudle Glen Railway, if operating. 3 May 1998 *(Sara Goodwins)*

A view from the other side of the car showing the good turn out of passengers. Car 1 is in the historic livery of the 'Douglas & Laxey Coast Electric Tramway' which it would have carried before the Ramsey extension opened. Douglas is about a fifteen minute ride away from Groudle. 3 May 1998

On leaving Groudle Glen the line swings right making an almost 180 degree turn over the viaduct to start the long climb up the north side of the glen. Road users, whether by tram or motor vehicle, often don't realise that the viaduct they're crossing rises to a height of around 100 ft above the stream. The trees look small from the road, but they are not! As the road and the railway were built together, this was open country and Eskadale is the only stop for the mile or so between Groudle Glen and Halfway. Originally a toll was payable by road users; the toll house was by Groudle Glen at the Douglas side of the viaduct.

Interestingly 'Eskadale' and 'Groudle' have the same Norse root but have evolved in different ways. In Old Norse *Escadala* means Clay Dale. By the early sixteenth century Clay Dale had become Crawdale; 250 years later it was Crowdale, and by 1860 it was Growdale and hence Groudle. Groudle Beach was once known as Escadalavik; as a *vik* is a creek, so the beach was Clay Dale Creek. The large house by the Eskadale stop, which once had a topiary peacock outside, is reputed to have been owned and occupied by Richard Maltby Broadbent (see page 27). Here we see winter saloon 20 with trailer 40 passing the stop southbound towards Groudle. 5 May 2002 *(Sara Goodwins)*

Winter saloon 20 again, although the livery has been changed from the fully lined-out style to the 1950s economy style with the title on the rocker panels amended to the terse 'M.E.R' form seen here. The blossoming cherry looks very fine but the garden hedge bordering the track makes the sightlines to the road extremely poor. Trailer 47 brings up the rear of the car set as it climbs north.

The tram stop is at pole 147 by Bibaloe Beg Road. Bibaloe Beg and Bibaloe Mooar are two farms above Onchan Village. Bibaloe Mooar is also called Ballastowell, but this has nothing to do with the stop of the same name just outside Ramsey (see page 131). Bibaloe Glen or Walk is a path along a stream from Molly Quirk's Glen and was formed when the Douglas to Laxey road was built in the nineteenth century cutting off the glen from the rest of the farm. 13 May 2005

This stop at pole 179 has a confusing number of aliases. Halfway along the main road built in the 1860s from Douglas to Laxey (now the A2), the original coaching inn was the Prince of Wales. Now the role of offering refreshment to travellers is fulfilled by the Liverpool Arms. Baldromma is the name of two farms, Baldromma Mooar and Baldromma Beg (big and little Baldromma respectively) accessed from the small road which emerges onto the main road by the postbox (see below). The name comes from *balley drommey*, *balley* meaning farm and *drommey* meaning 'belonging to the back', thus backbone or ridge. In English they would probably be known as Upper and Lower Ridge Farm.

The original Halfway House shelter was moved to Minorca some time ago (see page 67). The current shelter is a modern green-painted steel and glass design, similar to many others along the line, which doubles as a shelter for the main road buses. From this point northwards the tramway runs beside the A2 main road until the village of Baldrine.

Winter saloon 19 and trailer 40 approach the stop from Eskadale. 8 May 2008

On the other side of the tracks from the shelter is a Request Stop sign and one the Victorian post boxes that were installed at many points along the line. The lane which runs to Baldromma farms crosses the tram tracks and climbs to the right of the postbox. 18 May 2012

Scarffe's Crossing (pole 193) is the first of the halts beside the main A2 road between Halfway and Baldrine. It was designed to serve the local farms and Scarffe was the name of a prominent local farmer. Ballaskerroo, just up the hill to the north west, means Scarffe's Farm. *Balla*, sometimes *Balley*, means farm or homestead and, not surprisingly in an agricultural area, is a common prefix to Manx place names.

Scarffe might derive from *Skarð* which is a common surname in Iceland. *Skarð* means a gap or notch in Norse and is often used to describe a mountain pass. In addition *Skarð* is a name for a cormorant, also derived from the Scandinavian.

On 21 April 1798, William Scarffe married Ellinor Gelling in Lonan church. The Gelling family still own and run the free-range egg farm next to the tram stop and a small shop here sells the hens' output. The Gellings also have free-range pigs in the woodland next to the line. Anyone for a free-range bacon and egg breakfast?

This morning tunnel car 9 and trailer 43 had made an early morning run to Laxey and were returning to Douglas before normal service commenced. This was probably a driver training expedition when care is taken not to impede the passenger service. After the training session the car set can then be released for passenger use. 15 May 2012

Approaching from the other direction is car 5 which has clearly been the subject of a repaint in the previous winter. The wheel tyres showing white rims and the high standard of overall finish make the car a pleasure to see. Trailer 47 is coupled behind.

Both car 5 and trailer 47 are very well loaded. Indeed there was only standing room available on the car until Laxey, when a mass exodus for the Snaefell Mountain Railway relieved the pressure on space. 15 May 2012

Ballameanagh (pole 199) is the next wayside halt and is again named after the farms the stop was designed to serve. The road leading to them, across the road from the tramstop, is called Baŷr Balley Meanagh, which means Road of The Middle Farm – *meanagh* is middle in Manx. There are two middle farms, Ballameanagh Mooar and Ballameanagh Beg, the big and little one respectively. This is also the road leading to Lonan Old Church.

An alternative explanation for the meaning behind the name is that Ballameanagh could derive from *balley ny maynagh*, meaning the farm of the monks, with *meanagh* being substituted after the rarer word became even less common.

Thomas Mylechreest, who lived at Ballameanagh during the 1880s, was a member of the building committee which erected the Primitive Methodist chapel in Baldrine, adjacent to the next stop along the line.

Tunnel car 6 with trailer 41 approaches the stop with the first car of the day on its way northwards to Ramsey. 16 May 2012

Baldrine (pole 215) is a contraction of *balley drine*, meaning blackthorn farm. Here the MER rails run over land previously owned by Baroose Farm. The village itself was once known as Garwick, which is now more associated with the glen to the north of the stop and the bay reached by a steep descent.

The old Baldrine Primitive Methodist chapel is below the tram tracks near the tram stop and was built in 1843. One of the trustees was Robert Casement, more famous as the man behind the construction of the Lady Isabella water wheel in Laxey. When the new chapel was built in 1885, the old chapel became the Sunday School building and still claims to be the only hall suitable for church meetings in Lonan parish. As such it is often hired out for functions.

Here we see winter saloon 19 heading southwards across the level crossing just before the stop and the shelter. 6 May 2004

The waiting hut at Baldrine is looking very smart in this view, although the sign could do with repainting. The small plaque below the left hand window reads 'Garden created and tended by Baldrine WI from 1991'; the bolder notice on the other window is an unusually stern admonition not to trespass on the railway. Note the postbox. From the earliest years the tramcars carried mail, at first by an *ad hoc* arrangement, but after 1903 by a formal agreement. Not only was mail carried, often in a van behind the car or trailer, but the conductors were sworn in as auxiliary postmen. Their duties included emptying the lineside boxes, such as this one. Sadly the arrangement came to an end on 30 September 1975 when the MER service was curtailed at Laxey, and since then the mail has travelled by road van. Many but not all of the lineside boxes are still in use. 9 May 2007

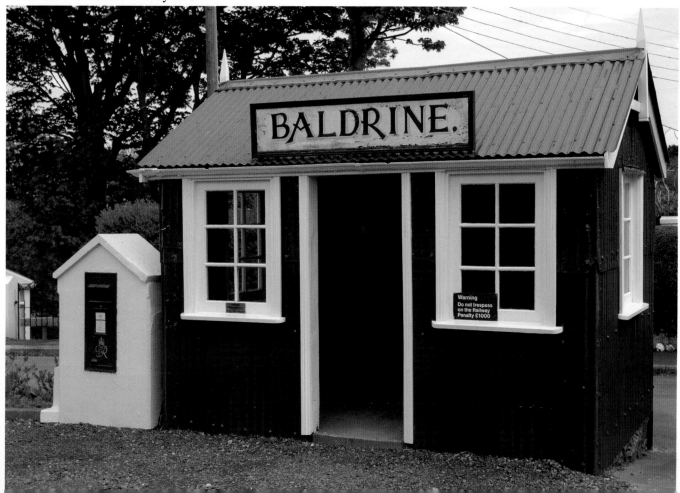

Inside the well-appointed shelter we find a waiting passenger. Seven-day rover ticket in hand with the island bus and rail timetable and a large-scale map we can deduce that this is a visitor rather than a local inhabitant. The shelter, with its comfortable bench seating, is a welcome resting place.

Visible through the window is the standard warning to motorists of an unfenced tram crossing. The signs are internationally-recognised standard pictures for trams despite them looking nothing like the MER cars depicted on the stop signs. On most other systems the tramcar outlines on the road signs would now look old fashioned, but here they post date the operating vehicles by several decades. 9 May 2007

Car 5 and trailer 40 form a southbound service which has stopped to pick up at Baldrine. Looking closely at the rocker panel on the car we can read *Raad-Yiarn Lectragh Vannin*, the Manx equivalent of the more prosaic 'Manx Electric Railway'. As in many languages 'Railway' becomes 'Road of Iron' in the indigenous tongue. 9 May 2007

Very little now remains to show that Garwick Glen (pole 244) was once a popular and bustling tourist destination. At one time there was a thatched kiosk selling tourist souvenirs, an array of flagpoles and a station building similar in size to that at Groudle Glen. It held a waiting room, manned booking office, station master's office and toilets.

All the buildings have now gone. The only remnants are the gateway that leads to the overgrown footpath down to the main road, and the crossover where cars could be turned back to handle the heavy traffic on busy days.

Car 5 leaves Garwick Glen single motor heading inland and towards Douglas. Passengers can look down into the glen once owned by the MER – the only way the public can now see it. The large white building is now a private dwelling, but was once the Garwick Glen Hotel. Tourists alighting at Garwick Glen could take tea in the gardens, enjoy the maze and rockwork fountains or visit the smugglers' caves on the beach as well as play tennis. 6 May 2004

This is the crossover in the track where cars were reversed when needed. The pointwork is still available for use when single line working is in operation and the crossover wiring is also in place. A path leads down from the tracks here to the main road in Baldrine Village and it is possible to make the walk down to the delightful Port Garwick, where trees grow on the beach.

The part of the glen above the road was called Garwick Glen, after the village, whilst the part below the road was Glen Gawne (or Cowin) after the Gawne family who owned or lived in it several hundred years ago. The stream is called the River Gawne and enters the sea at Port Garwick. As noted previously the village is now called Baldrine; an area of many identities! 5 October 2013

Winter saloon 21 arrives at Garwick Glen with a northbound service. The car has just turned sharp right across the head of the glen, the very tight curve causing a squeal of protest from the wheel flanges. 5 October 2013

Ballagawne (pole 257) can be translated from the Manx as 'Gawne's Farm': *balla* is of course farm and Gawne is the family name. Gawne must have been a common Manx surname as there are Ballagawne Farms in Arbory, Michael and Rushen as well as this one in Lonan.

In this view we see an unusual car set heading north away from the photographer. Open motor car 32 of 1906 is leading lightweight open trailer number 51 painted in the original 1893 livery. This is not a normal service but a special working.

As at many other stops the waiting shelter comprises a modern green painted steel and glass fabrication, which doubles as a bus shelter for northbound buses on the adjacent main road. Separate facilities are provided for southbound buses. 6 May 2004

An unusual view of the Ballagawne stop and its surrounding area taken from the Clay Head Road. A southbound service comprising winter saloon 21 and open trailer 42 is approaching the stop.

In the background is Lonan All Saints Church, built in 1834 and not to be confused with the much older Lonan Old Church near Ballameanagh (see page 32). In it is a memorial to Colour Sergeant William Wallace of the 2nd Battalion Seaforth Highlanders, killed in action at Paardeberg, during the Boer War in South Africa in 1900. The memorial states that he was the son of John Wallace, headmaster of Ballagawne Board School. However, both *Smith's Commercial Directory* of 1883 and *Brown's Directory* of 1881 list William Wallace as schoolmaster at Ballagawne, so either William helped his father, or the memorial is mistaken about his father's name.

Also just discernible on the right is the road crossing at Ballabeg where the tramway crosses over the A2 at a light controlled crossing. 13 May 2005 *(Sara Goodwins)*

Again looking north we can see that the tramway runs parallel to the main A2 road which is on the right. The houses in the distance are on the Ballacannell Estate just outside Laxey.

In the mid-nineteenth century nine acres of land at Ballagawne were owned by the Cowin family. Cowins had lived here since the seventeenth century as they appear in the 1643 manorial roll and Gawne is thought to be a corruption of Cowin.

Winter saloon 22 is approaching the stop. A garden hedge make the sight lines to the Ballagawne stop poor when heading north particularly for the crossing on the Creg ny Baa Road, but they're not too bad from this driver's point of view. *Creg ny Baa* means 'rock of the cows' and the Creg ny Baa pub, or, more accurately, the Keppel Hotel, is a noted landmark on the TT course. This is the back road to it. 8 May 2008

Ballabeg, pole 282, means 'little farm' and, not surprisingly, this is a common name across the island. When the MER track was laid through Ballabeg workmen discovered an old keeill and adjoining burial ground with a large number of lintel graves, although nothing now remains of this site. The keeill was thought to be dedicated to St Callan, a celtic saint from Ireland, and gave rise to the local name Kilkellan, often shortened to Killan. The name of the stream which runs under the MER track is Strooan ny Carlane, or 'stream of Callan'.

Two years after the burial ground was discovered, a wooden cross with the words 'Ancient Graves – *Kist Vaens*' was erected to mark the site. It stood next to a low wall topped with white stones which ran alongside the MER embankment.

The old Parochial School, better known as the 'Clerk's School', was next to the site of the keeill and locals spoke of human remains often being dug up in this area. 7 May 2007

Winter saloon 19 (above) has just crossed the main A2 road. Trailer 46 is not visible but is following on behind. A few years ago there were peacocks living wild in this area, presumably introduced by one of the residents. 7 May 2007

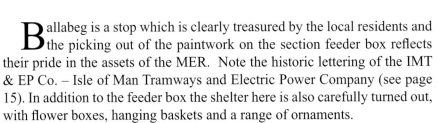

Ballabeg is a stop which is clearly treasured by the local residents and the picking out of the paintwork on the section feeder box reflects their pride in the assets of the MER. Note the historic lettering of the IMT & EP Co. – Isle of Man Tramways and Electric Power Company (see page 15). In addition to the feeder box the shelter here is also carefully turned out, with flower boxes, hanging baskets and a range of ornaments.

Ballabeg is adjacent to the light-controlled crossing of the main coast road, where the tramway swings away from the road to make an almost right-angled crossing and then resumes a roughly parallel path once on the other side; in the top photograph car 19 has just made this manoeuvre. Prior to the installation of the lights a crossing keeper warned travellers on the main road of the approach of trams. 20 May 2010

From Fairy Cottage (pole 307) it's downhill all the way to Laxey. Here tunnel car 9 and trailer 47 are about to pause at at the stop on the way north. 20 May 2010

The Fairy Cottage stop lies just off the main coast road of Pinfold Hill and the waiting hut can be glimpsed between the houses as seen here. The 'Private' sign on the gate shows that this is not the pedestrian access to the line which is a short distance downhill.

'Fairy' and 'Cottage' are English words – the Manx normally refer to fairies as 'themselves'. It is possible that the name derives from the Manx word *faaie* meaning 'a well-manured field near a manor house', or possibly *faare* meaning 'near'. Whether the name comes from a Manx or English source it seems likely that it refers to a specific building.

While no sightings of the little people have been recorded at Fairy Cottage, it was the place where a UFO was seen. In May 1984 a couple looking out of their house at Fairy Cottage over the darkness of Laxey Bay saw a flat disc-like flying object with bright headlights and several side lights hover over the water before flying over Snaefell. 7 May 2007

The shelter provides respite from the rain, which, judging by the passenger's mac., is obviously falling (as it sometimes does on the island...). Each of the old-style shelters has a charm of its own which is sadly lacking in the steel and glass offerings of the twenty-first century. Although the practice is discouraged, they have also been known to provide emergency overnight accommodation for TT visitors. 11 September 2011

There is a long slow climb from Laxey to Ballabeg and Fairy Cottage is about half way. Here winter saloon 21 with trailer 40 tackles the climb, leaving the Laxey Bay behind. 20 May 2010

The MER has tended to be conservative in its approach to trackwork and permanent way, relying on proven technology. The standard construction used flat bottom rails directly spiked to the wooden sleepers and was still used well into the first decade of the twenty-first century.

When the crossover at Fairy Cottage was relaid in early 2009 it was an early application of construction using steel baseplates between the foot of the rail and the sleeper and pandrol rail fastenings. This form of construction had been used on UK standard gauge lines since the 1960s.

Still showing the engineers' construction marks the new crossover at Fairy Cottage shows that more modern forms of trackwork were not automatically debarred. In 2012 some replacement track between Groudle Glen and Groudle Old Road has incorporated concrete sleepers as well as pandrol rail clips. 18 May 2009

Open motor 16 is seen at Preston's Crossing (pole 312) heading towards Douglas before normal service one morning. Evidently the car is in the charge of the engineers and not in normal service. This early-season view is one of the 'drying out' runs to Laxey and back to remove the winter condensation from the motors before the influx of visitors. Behind the car the houses on the hill show the route of the Ramsey Road as it climbs out of Laxey. Below the road and parallel with it, the route of the MER is much more difficult to pick out.

Alone of the 14-18 batch of cars, car 16 is equipped with Bush D type bogies and is the sole serviceable car of this batch of five. 12 May 2005

Tunnel car 6 and trailer 40 have stopped at Preston's Crossing with a southbound service and are just pulling away up the hill towards Fairy Cottage.

The crossing probably takes its name from George Corlett Preston who was the headmaster of the South Cape School for forty years. He was born at Ballaugh in 1857 and educated on the Isle of Man; as a locally-educated academic his advice on the provision of education was frequently sought by various government committees. Elected to the House of Keys for Garff Sheading 1922-4 Mr Preston had a long record of public service as clerk to the Laxey Village Commissioners as well as working for local Friendly Societies.

Preston's Crossing is on Old Laxey Hill. Running close to it is Old School Hill. Did Mr Preston regularly cross the tram tracks here on his way to and from work? Whether he did or not, the name of the halt seems an obvious nod to a local worthy. 17 May 2010

At Preston's Crossing, Old Laxey Hill crosses the tramway at an oblique angle on its descent from New Road to Old Laxey. The line runs almost parallel to Old Laxey Hill immediately before Preston's Crossing and poor sight lines mean that a good look out is needed by both rail and road users.

The houses in the foreground on the sea side of Old Laxey Hill are perched on the edge of the cliff. The views over the Ushtairs (the name given to some small rocks at the south end of Laxey beach) are tremendous but the situation may be a worry to residents; cliff falls have been known in the area.

Taken from across the Laxey valley from the Minorca tram stop, car 19 and trailer 40 have completed their detour inland to cross the valley and have now climbed the southern flank on their way back to Douglas. 3 April 2011

Seen heading north is rebuilt car 7 with trailer 46. Immediately after this photograph was taken, car 7's trolley left the overhead wire and the motorman needed to bring the car to a swift halt. The reverse curvature at the crossing can set up undesirable sideways forces on the trolley wheel, which is another reason for caution at this point.

The shelter in the distance to the right of the picture is the one at Fairy Cottage; the two stops are not far apart. Also in the background, this time to the left, is a fuchsia bush in flower. Fuchsia bushes grow wild all over the island and many large specimens can be seen along the line. They can be spectacular in the flowering season and obviously like the climate. 11 September 2011

An oddity in the overhead wiring at Preston's Crossing above the northbound line. The nearer support follows the normal suspension below the bracket arm. The additional pull-off on the Douglas side of the traction pole gives a somewhat less abrupt change of curvature just before the road crossing. Obviously the intention is to prevent the sort of de-poling that occurred with car 7 (left). 8 May 2007 (*Sara Goodwins*)

Before the morning service has started we see an industrial diesel propelling the tower wagon mounted on the underframe of trailer 52 across Preston's Crossing towards Laxey. The two men are looking away from the camera as the driver's view of the track is obscured by the works car and his colleague is signalling to him. Overhead line works must have been necessary and on arrival at Laxey the vehicles will shunt clear of the line to allow the first northbound service car to pass. Note the cabledrum of overhead wire mounted on the nearer end of number 52. The tower wagon will be seen shortly afterwards in Laxey Station (page 62). 22 May 2009

Car 1 of the 'Douglas & Laxey Coast Electric Tramway' is seen on Preston's Crossing. This photograph was taken on the day after the view of car 16 (see page 41). Today it is car 1's turn to have the early morning drying out run to Laxey and back. The main difference is that the photographer was not up quite as early as the previous day and only managed this view by a spirited run up Old Laxey Hill. An interesting view, but a breather needed at the top! 13 May 2005

DOUGLAS & LAXEY COAST ELECTRIC TRAMWAY.

South Cape (pole 320) overlooks Laxey Bay and obviously gets its name as it is the cape which is south of the harbour entrance. It is at this point that the line turns up the Laxey valley.

Heading north blue-liveried car 2 and winter trailer 57 are an unusual sighting. This is a special photographic charter and the car set is running ahead of the first service car of the day. Sadly the weather has not been kind to either the tram charterers or to the driver who cannot escape the rain on the open-fronted motor car. The Manx weather can be very changeable (!) and a later view on this day will show the car set in less dreary conditions (see page 97). 6 May 2004

Heading south on a sunny spring day are winter saloon 22 and trailer 41. They have completed the climb up from Laxey along the south side of the valley and now the tramway turns to run parallel to the coast. The gradient also eases from 1 in 40 to 1 in 89, according to the design profile. On the extreme left and level with the trailer's roof valencing can just be seen the waiting shelter at Minorca on the far side of the Laxey valley adjacent to the viaduct over Minorca Hill.

The coming of the tramway brought increased prosperity to the area and had a knock-on effect on house prices and revenue from building land. On New Year's Day 1898 the *Isle of Man Examiner* commented that building plots at South Cape had '... building sites adjoining the main road in front and within a few yards of the tramway. There is good stone in the field adjoining and also sand near so that building material is ready to hand without much cost.' South Cape was one of the poorer parts of Laxey and home to many of the miners who worked in the area. 7 May 2008

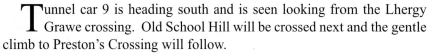

Tunnel car 9 is heading south and is seen looking from the Lhergy Grawe crossing. Old School Hill will be crossed next and the gentle climb to Preston's Crossing will follow.

During the early part of the twentieth century, William Valentine Worthington lived at South Cape and worked as schoolmaster under George Preston, after whom Preston's Crossing is probably named (see page 41). 14 September 2011

Photographed from a passing tram, as can be seen from the shadows on the track, the sign by the waiting shelter at South Cape confirms that this is the nearest stop to Laxey Beach and Promenade. There is a steep drop down to sea level so the return walk is not quite such easy going. Previously the sign included the wording 'Keep Your Seats for Laxey'; it would have been disappointing to get off here and not find the connecting Snaefell car awaiting.

Prior to 1929 the beach at Laxey extended as far as Back Shore Road. Laxey Promenade was constructed in 1929 to relieve unemployment among ex-miners and the current beach café was originally a store owned by Laxey mines. In 1859 the store was loaned to the Methodists for use as a temporary chapel whilst their Wesleyan chapel in Glen Road was being rebuilt.

On the skyline, to the right of the picture, can be seen the traction poles of the MER above the opposite headland (which is not, however, called North Cape). The tramway runs inland along the valley to Laxey and climbs back on the other side of the river to reach the point seen here. The long detour means that the north headland is about ten minutes away by tram, but a lot closer as the crow flies. 20 May 2009

Winter saloon 20 and trailer 47 (left) head north on another less than idyllic day. The photographer was in the doorway of the shelter as can be seen from the hanging basket bracket on the left. Unusually South Cape is not situated at a road crossing, but positioned midway between two. At the south end Old School Hill breaks its steep descent to cross the tracks, whilst at the Laxey end Lhergy Grawe makes an oblique crossing.

A tarmac path (see to the left of car 9, upper picture on page 46) leads to the shelter from either crossing, and signs point to the stop location. The arrangement is surprising as the MER frequently has very closely spaced stops often crossing roads; perhaps the sightlines were too poor to allow cars to stop at either or both of the road crossings. 19 May 2010

There have been no fewer than three car sheds on this site. The first was constructed in 1904 and had four roads. Sadly this became the site of one of the worst blows ever to strike the railway as it was totally destroyed by fire early in the morning of Saturday 5 April 1930. Motor cars 3, 4, 8 and 24, together with trailers 34, 35, 38, 39, 40, 41 and 44 were also lost in the inferno. Two other trailers were manhandled out of the shed and repaired. The motor

cars were never replaced but three replacement trailers taking the numbers 40, 41 and 44, were supplied by English Electric in the following year, and are all still in service.

To replace the car shed destroyed by fire tramway historians state that a steel frame structure clad in corrugated iron was constructed in 1931, although the plate on the main doors (see inset) stated that it was built a year earlier. The ravages of the weather led to severe corrosion and by 2002 the roof was deemed to be in danger of collapse. Most of the stored trams were moved to the former Homefield bus depot in Douglas and the shed roof removed. Here winter saloon 20 and trailer 46 pass the decidedly decrepit remains of the roofless shed on their way to Ramsey. 13 September 2006

This stop (pole 345) is located where a footpath leading from New Road to the valley crosses the line by the car shed. The site of Laxey car shed was the location of the first Laxey station, opened on 28 July 1894 when the original line was extended from Groudle Glen to Laxey. The major structure on the extension is the viaduct over Groudle Glen itself. Simultaneously the original line between Derby Castle and Groudle had been upgraded from single to double track and the additional four route miles installed. To work the greatly extended line six totally enclosed motor cars (numbers 4 to 9) and six trailers were added to the fleet. The new line of the Douglas & Laxey Coast Electric Tramway made travel between the two towns much more practicable. The tram fare was one shilling which was a massive reduction on the stage coach fare of eleven shillings.

Here winter saloon 21 passes the third car shed, which finally opened in 2009, and the stop on its way north on a dull day near the end of the 2013 season. 6 October 2013

The interior view of the second (1931) Laxey car shed shows the lack of protection from the elements that resulted from the removal of the roof. The pile of corrugated iron over the right hand side track is the remains of much of the roof which was dumped on the floor. The shed had been cleared of the majority of the rolling stock five years before the date of the photograph. Standing behind the door at the far end is tunnel car 7 which at the time was in a very poor state of repair and, considered unfit for passenger use, continued to be employed as the works car.

At the nearer end of the same track as car 7 is a Ruston diesel locomotive owned by RMS Locotec (number H048) which was employed on permanent way works on the MER for some years. This engine is also unprotected from the elements. 9 May 2007

A year later finds the shed still roofless, but the sole occupant is MER diesel-electric locomotive 34. The vehicle is an interesting hybrid and started life working on the Snaefell Mountain Railway. Low voltage DC current such as is used to power the trams cannot be fed over a long distance so, when the Snaefell line was built in 1895, the voltage drop over the length of the line was such that feeding current solely from Laxey would have been inadequate. A power station was therefore provided just below the Bungalow Station near the line's mid-point, the remains of which can still be seen today. Snaefell car 7, also known as *Maria*, was a goods tram with a cab at each end and was used to ferry coal to the power station. With advances in electricity supply it became possible to feed high voltage AC current from Laxey to the power station building, now used as an electricty substation, where it was transformed to DC to feed the wires. The freight tram *Maria* was therfore no longer needed for transporting fuel.

In 1995 *Maria* was resurrected for the Snaefell centenary. Several years later she was substantially rebuilt and fitted with MER 3'-0" bogies and a diesel generator. As such she is now her own mobile power station. Renumbered as MER car 34, a number unused since trailer 34 was lost in the Laxey car shed of 1930, and complete with high visibility end panels and bright yellow paint, *Maria* can operate whether the power is on or not. She made her first forays in 2008, can haul a trailing load and is a useful addition to the engineering team's workforce. 5 May 2008

Before the roof of the shed was removed, a number of individual retrieval exercises took place. Here tunnel car 6 has extracted trailer 36 from the shed and has shunted it onto the northbound track. The trolley pole will be swung round and the ensemble will use the crossover directly in front of car 6 to take the line to Douglas. At about nine o'clock in the morning, it is well before the first service car is due to arrive. Care is always taken with moving stock which has been stationary for a long time so hopefully arrival in Douglas will not interfere with normal operations. As seen on page 11 car 36 could be seen at Derby Castle the following day as it awaited the final stage of its journey to Homefield.

After the roof of the shed had been removed, the sidings inside it were used to store a small amount of rolling stock deemed essential for engineering work. Although out of sight and safe from unauthorised interference, the weather protection was non-existent and regrettably car 7, which was the engineering car for most of the first decade of the twenty-first century, suffered considerable damage while based here (see page 49). 7 May 2002

Parked at the Laxey end of the third car shed, and almost directly opposite the stop itself, is freight wagon number 8, loaded with sleepers and other material from its use in engineering works. In earlier days the MER had considerable freight traffic and a number of vans and open wagons still survive around the system.

At the time of writing a small selection of restored vehicles is visible at Laxey Station near the goods shed. 18 April 2010

The current Laxey Station (pole 359) is located in the centre of the village and provides an easy interchange between the MER and the Snaefell Mountain Railway (SMR).

As noted on page 48, the original MER station was situated where the car shed was subsequently built. During 1895 work had progressed on the building of the Snaefell Mountain Railway, but the original terminus of this line was where the current (mountain) car shed is so interchange between the two lines required an inconveniently long walk. The plan was to extend the MER to Ramsey, but in order to do this substantial engineering works were needed in the Laxey area. Firstly Glen Roy needed to be bridged, which was achieved by the stone viaduct which parallels the New Road viaduct downstream of the

Laxey flour mill. The line then reached to the current station. By extending the Snaefell line down the hill a shared station resulted which eliminated the annoying distance between the two railways. Even making this extension to the mountain line was done in two stages with a terminus by Ham and Egg Terrace (Dumbell's Row) being in use for a short time.

Laxey Station now retains a 1930s air. The painting of the name on station roofs was common at that time as an aid to aviators. The Second World War put a stop to that practice in general, as aiding the Luftwaffe's navigation was not such a good idea. Being so far beyond the reach of most enemy aircraft of the time, Laxey continued the practice and it adds a period touch to the station.

Laxey, which in Manx is *Laxaa* or salmon river, is the most important station along the line and, in addition to providing interchange facilities with the SMR, the town is an important tourist centre in its own right. 20 May 2010

The Snaefell cars normally wait for the cars from Douglas to arrive as they often carry most of the SMR's passengers. Visitors staying in Laxey can board first and here we see winter saloon 21 (there is also a trailer behind) approaching across the Glen Roy viaduct. The photographer has picked his seat on the mountain car to take this different view. 21 May 2009

During the early part of the 2008 season the line between Laxey and Ramsey was closed for remedial renewal of some of the permanent way. Normally the winter saloons provide a through service and it is not common to find a short working from Douglas terminating here with such a car. Car 22, with a replica body constructed in 1992, has switched to the Douglas bound line and its trailer (41) is making its way over the crossover to join it.

On the left are two of the Snaefell cars. Car 5, on the left, differs from the other cars in that the bodywork does not feature the clerestory, shown on car 2 next to it. Snaefell car 5, like MER car 22, was a fire victim. On 16 August 1970 car 5 had reached Snaefell summit when an electrical fault started a fire. In the high winds the body was severely damaged. The replacement body seen here was constructed by H D Kinnin of Ramsey, and, while following the general appearance of the other five cars, the absence of the clerestory is most noticeable. When initially rebuilt the car was fitted with bus-style sliding aluminium window vents, which were replaced with windows which matched the other moutain cars during a major overhaul in the late 1990s. At the time of writing, the joiners who built the new body are still trading and it is not unusual to see their van parked in Walpole Road, Ramsey, adjacent to the MER line as it enters the town.

Snaefell car 2 is representative of the majority of the fleet. A batch of six cars were supplied for the opening of the line in 1895 and these have served ever since. Regular services have only ever been provided in the summer as this is purely a tourist line. In 2013 Snaefell car 1 appeared in a blue and white livery following a major overhaul. 7 May 2008

Tunnel car 6, with twin droplights on the end of the body is waiting in Laxey Station with a northbound service for Ramsey. At Laxey the conductors report the number of passengers arriving and departing on the car to the station master. The car leaves only when the station master has given his approval. 10 May 1998

The Snaefell line has a gradient of 1 in 12 for much of its length and, as an extra safety feature, a centre rail is provided for additional braking capacity. This is the Fell system, patented by the inventor in 1863. In order to accommodate the braking gear, the gauge is 3'-6" rather than the normal island gauge of 3'-0". For many years the Snaefell cars were overhauled at Derby Castle. The car bodies were transferred between their Snaefell trucks and spare MER trucks and then towed to and from Douglas by a MER motor car. The practice ceased when a replacement Snaefell depot was constructed with the capacity to overhaul the bodies locally.

The interesting piece of trackwork (left) shows the Snaefell track splitting into two sidings on the left. The narrower MER track is to the right and the siding in the foreground trails onto the northbound MER line. Looking similar to a pair of points there is no absolute choice of direction, which is decided by the gauge of the vehicle and the position of the single swinging point blade on the right.

This piece of permanent way was removed after the close of the 2013 season when the trackwork in Laxey station was completely renewed over the winter of 2013-4. 16 May 2012

The Snaefell line generates a high volume of traffic to and from Douglas. Accordingly cars are frequently turned at Laxey to cope with the demand. Here winter saloon 20 approaches from Ramsey on the southbound line whilst open motor car 26 waits beyond the crossover on the northbound line. 26's trolley pole has already been turned and, once 20 has loaded at Laxey and departed for Douglas, car 26 will reverse over the crossover to form the next southbound service. A short wait may be necessary for the passengers from Snaefell to cross the tracks and board. 10 May 1996

Oops! In the early twenty-first century a set of stop flags was produced and installed along the line. Using them, passengers would be in no doubt about where to wait for the next car. The termini hardly needed the additional signage and, with its name proclaimed in large capitals on the roof of the station building, nor did Laxey. Unfortunately the sign itself proclaims this to be 'Laxey Sation'! 8 May 2002

Car 9 was initially fitted with its myriad lights and advertising boxes for the 1993 'Year of Railways' celebrations, including the MER centenary. A number of other notable dates were commemorated in the next few years and the displays were subtly altered to mark the centenary of the Snaefell Mountain Railway (1995), 125 years since the Isle of Man Railway's first line between Douglas and Peel opened (1998) and, as shown here, the year 2000 celebrations which assure us of the 'Manx Electric Railway – Back to the Future', albeit with a blank car-end display. Although the MER is considered fantastic by many enthusiasts, the journey to Ramsey is unlikely to be as futuristic as the science fiction film of the same name.

Standing by the front steps of car 9 is Ian Ewan, for many years the Laxey Stationmaster. 11 May 2000

In the days when the MER provided a goods service the corrugated iron goods shed provided at the Ramsey end of the station was used to load and unload wagons under cover. Adjacent to the shed was a siding which was frequently used to store a car set during the day.

Open motor car 32 and trailer 62 were both delivered in 1906 and represent the last major purchase of new cars for the MER. Normal practice when parking a tram is to turn the trolley pole so that the car is ready for its next move: for some reason this has not been done this time. 2 May 2004

Traffic on the Snaefell line is dependent on the weather and on a fine day extra cars are run from Douglas to Laxey for those wishing to make the ascent. Having run round the trailer the motor car can then reverse into the siding and wait for the rush back to Douglas as the mountain cars return their passengers from the summit. In a quiet moment on a sunny afternoon we find car 6 (now with a single windscreen, see page 7) with trailer 43 parked in the siding awaiting its next tour of duty. 7 May 2007

Car 9 again, but late in the afternoon where a welcome splash of colour is added by the car's external light bulbs. This is the last car to Ramsey tonight. The external illuminated boxes have been removed from car 9 since we saw it on the previous page; obviously 2003 did not have any special significance or anniversaries to commemorate. 4 May 2003

Heading towards Ramsey is car 6 with lightweight trailer 60. This trailer is finished in the 1950s nationalized green and white livery which is generally accepted as being unpopular, although it looks bright and cheerful enough. The trailer is more often to be found running with similarly liveried open motor number 16. Despite this being a bright spring day there are few takers for seats on the trailer. The lightweight trailers have fewer full-height uprights and so no possibility of shutters. Passengers therefore have no way of keeping out the weather. Perhaps there is a biting wind today? 6 May 2003

Car 26 has arrived at Laxey following its drying-out run at the start of the season. Car 26 will shortly run beyond the crossover and reverse in order to make its way back to Douglas.

Cars 24-27 were initially trailers and arrived with motor cars 14-18 in 1898. In 1903 they were equipped with motor bogies and fitted with a set of stepped running boards to clear the axle boxes (see page 53). As a result they were nicknamed 'paddleboxes'. Car 24 was lost in the Laxey car shed fire. The others still exist but at the time of writing none is serviceable. 7 May 2004

It is a quiet morning in Laxey and car 1, in its historic livery, is about to start back for Douglas. This is early in the season and the car is on a drying out run and not in passenger service. The car is looking a little care worn with a dented dash and the roof paintwork has seen better days. However the MER tries to look after its assets and, as can be seen from the picture of the car at Preston's Crossing a year later (see page 44), a full repaint was carried out over the next winter. Cars 1 and 2, the open motors, and the closed trailers have metal end dashes, whereas the bodywork of all other cars and trailers are built entirely of wood. 7 May 2004

The use of the siding by the Laxey goods shed for day-time storage has already been noted on pages 54 and 55. Here we see car 20 pushing trailer 46 into the siding. During this manoeuvre the conductor stands on the footboard at the leading end of the trailer and signals to the motorman that it is safe to proceed. Once the set is safely tucked away in the siding the crew can relax until their next call of duty. Normally the winter saloons are used on through services but on this Saturday late in the season car 20 has been called on for a less strenuous day of work.

As can be seen, there is little clearance between the tram and the Mines Tavern. For over fifty years this building was the house where the Laxey Mine Captain lived and part of the building had to be demolished when the electric railway was laid. They obviously didn't want to demolish more than absolutely necessary! 14 September 2013

Tunnel bar rather than tunnel car! Inside the Mines Tavern the bar is modelled on MER tramcar 9. Above the 'windows' is a rope bell pull reaching to a bell behind and above where the motorman would sit. But be careful! The person who rings this has to buy everyone a drink! Despite appearances, if you think the bar is moving like a tram you've probably had too many. 2 February 2014

For several years at the start of the twenty-first century, tunnel car 7 was used by the engineering team. During this time it was stored in the remains of the second Laxey car shed (see page 49), which left it exposed to the worst of the Manx weather.

Here a somewhat dishevelled car 7 is seen at Laxey Station on works duties, out and about before the first service car of the day. Trailer 52 is seen again, but this view predates the installation of the tower wagon mechanism and the wire reel holder seen opposite. 7 May 2003 *(Sara Goodwins)*

A tower wagon is normally kept at the Laxey car shed together with a motor car which can be used in engineering service. Open motor 27 is seen pushing a tower wagon through Laxey Station and onto the Glen Roy viaduct. Note that it has been fitted with a plastic windscreen, presumably to provide the motorman with some protection. It is early morning and the poles and wires team have been out and about before the first service car.

At this time car 27 was allocated to engineering duties and could seen around the system engaged in various tasks including weedkilling, permanent way and overhead works. 6 May 1996

On a journey from the north, the photographer's service car, the first car of the day from Ramsey, had passed car 32 with the tower wagon based on trailer 52 waiting at Ballaragh.

After the service car had passed, car 32 switched to the southbound line via the crossover and followed the service car down to Laxey. Here car 32 is passing through Laxey Station on its way to the car shed. There the engineering team shunted the set into the shed. 26 October 2013

On the last weekend of the MER's 2013 service a special photographers' day was arranged. Sadly the weather was typical of November with rain and dull grey skies doing little to provide stunning effects. The efforts of the staff were, however, enough to make up for the less than perfect lighting, and interesting car formations were run along the line, with special emphasis at Laxey.

This view shows original 1893 motor car 2 in Laxey Station with a goods wagon, illustrating the freight service which had been run on the MER in days long ago. Shunting the demonstration cars to avoid the still-running normal service added interest to the photographic opportunities. 2 November 2013

During the special photographers' event (see previous page), variety was the order of the day and, after it had shunted the goods wagon off to the sidings, car 2 made an excursion to the goods shed, where a couple of tower wagons had been stored. The shed itself is no longer wired so the trolley of car 2 was at a precarious angle onto the southbound wire (see inset picture) to perform this operation. Having collected the tower wagons these were then posed in Laxey Station for the photographers' delight.

The nearer vehicle, painted in yellow, is based on an MER van, and the farther one uses a wagon chassis for its running gear. Normally trailer 52 is used with its more up-to-date elevating platform and higher guard rails as seen in the view of car 32 (see

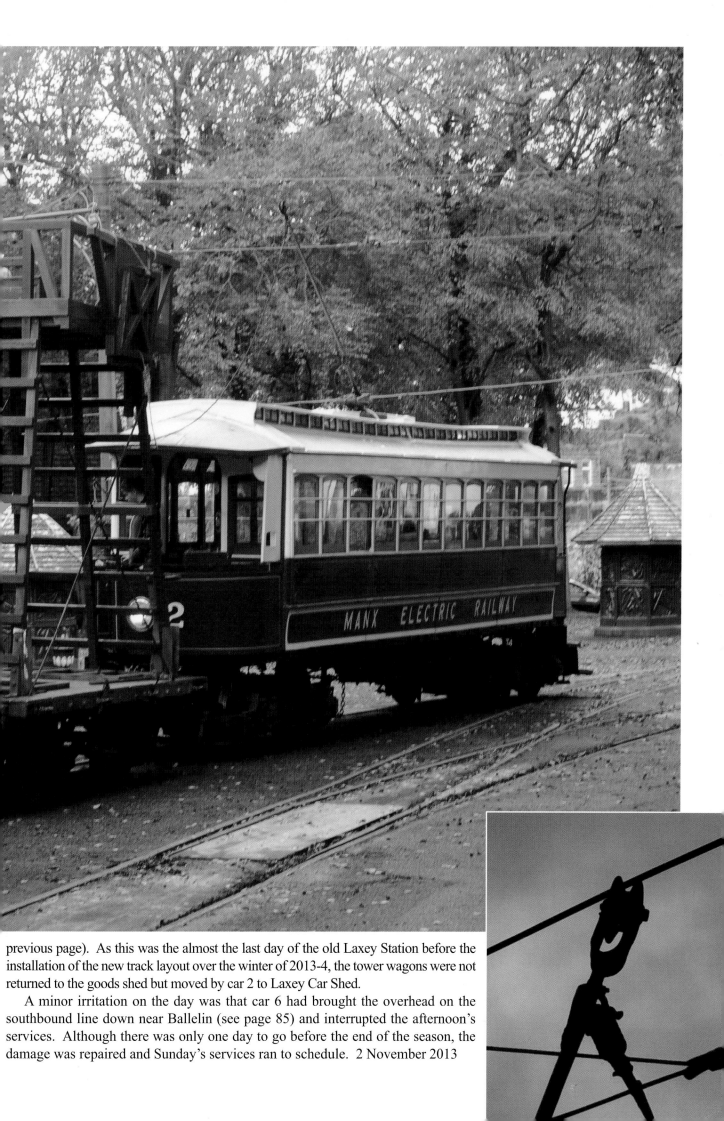

previous page). As this was the almost the last day of the old Laxey Station before the installation of the new track layout over the winter of 2013-4, the tower wagons were not returned to the goods shed but moved by car 2 to Laxey Car Shed.

A minor irritation on the day was that car 6 had brought the overhead on the southbound line down near Ballelin (see page 85) and interrupted the afternoon's services. Although there was only one day to go before the end of the season, the damage was repaired and Sunday's services ran to schedule. 2 November 2013

Diesel-electric locomotive 34 has already been seen lurking behind the doors of the Laxey car shed (see page 49). Here the locomotive is in Laxey Station and has been shunting a tower wagon into the goods shed. In 2008 number 34 was still a very new item on the MER rolling stock list. Finding her in Laxey Station was lucky for the photographer. The shiny new paint certainly brightened up a very dull day while waiting for the first service car to arrive from Douglas. 9 May 2008

Parked on the southbound running line in Laxey Station is the tower wagon and wire car, 52. This was seen earlier in the morning at Preston's Crossing when it was being propelled towards Laxey by a small diesel engine (see page 44). The engine has moved off, and trailer 52 will also be moved out of the way before the first southbound service car arrives.

Car 52 is one of the original 1893 trailers delivered for the opening of the line, and a sister of trailer 51 (see pages 36, 89 and 101 among others). This car has been used exclusively for engineering purposes for many years. 22 May 2009

During the celebrations of 125 years of the Isle of Man Railway, a number of events took place around the island. One of these was an evening event at Laxey Station featuring Isle of Man Railway number 1, *Sutherland*, together with the MER and Snaefell number 1s.

Many other interesting cars were brought to Laxey including open motor car 16 shown here on the northbound line. In the background, car 9, complete with special branding and with lights burning, can be seen near the Mines Tavern. *Sutherland* was coupled to MER winter trailer 58 and services operated to Fairy Cottage (see page 39). It's a steep climb for a 125-year-old steam engine! 7 May 1998 *(Sara Goodwins)*

The final view at Laxey is taken at 10:40 pm. It is a dark and rainy night but car 9 with its illuminations switched on is a welcoming sight, as is Laxey Station building with the warm and cosy waiting room still available. During the summer months, the MER and Snaefell Mountain Railway offer a service to take diners to the summit hotel for an evening meal. Car 9 has already made one trip to Douglas with the first group of diners taking winter trailer 57 along. It now awaits the final diners as they make their way down the mountain to return to Douglas.

Note that the illuminations on car 9 have been renewed. Rather than the multitude of individual light bulbs (see page 55) the new scheme uses tubes of LEDs for a rather different but still stunning effect. The sight of this car gliding apparently effortlessly through the Manx countryside at night is surreal and well worth looking out for. 18 May 2012

Dumbell's Row (pole 372) is also in Laxey Village and is the line of terraced housing built along Mines Road for the miners of Laxey in 1860. It is the island's longest line of purpose-built industrial housing under a continuous roof.

Although officially named Dumbell's Row the houses soon acquired the nickname of Ham and Egg Terrace when many of the residents opened their parlours to cater for visitors. Only the first house in the row, at the Laxey end, is still an eatery. Established in 1902, and known for almost a hundred years as Brown's Café, it is now called 'Laxey's'.

Here car 5 with trailer 40 pass the stop and are about to cross Laxey New Road on their way into Laxey Station. The end gable and chimney of Dumbell's Row is just visible above the trailer. The track on the left is the 3' 6" Snaefell Mountain Railway line which splits into two tracks behind car 5 and can be seen climbing round the corner. 7 May 2007

Car 6 with trailer 46 straddles Mines Road heading towards Ramsey having just the passed Dumbell's Row stop. The terrace was named after George William Dumbell, founder of the bank which notoriously crashed in 1900 plunging many of the businesses on the the Isle of Man, including the MER, into decades of financial problems. Dumbell had an interest in the Laxey mines which explains the naming of the houses.

Above the front half of car 6 can just be seen the top of the Lady Isabella water wheel about half a mile away. Also just creeping into the picture on the right is works trailer 52 on the siding which is on the inland side of the line here. With its easy access to the main road this is a useful area to transfer items such as rails or poles between lorries and works cars. 16 May 2009

This view is from the road above Laxey which climbs to the small village of Agneash known by locals as 'The City'. The line of terraced housing is Dumbell's Row fronting onto Mines Road. Above them is the car shed of the Snaefell Mountain Railway. In front of the Snaefell car shed is a small shed which is used to store the Wickham car used to service the radio station on Snaefell's summit. The tracks of the mountain line descend behind Dumbell's Row and emerge near the road crossing (see top picture opposite) where winter saloon 21 and trailer 42 are crossing New Road. Having started out from Laxey Station they are about to pass the stop at Dumbell's Row with a northbound service. 2 May 2004 *(Sara Goodwins)*

Minorca Station (pole 409) is situated on Minorca Hill on the north side of Old Laxey. Unusually for the MER the stop is considerably higher than the street level at this point. Just as on the opposite side of the valley, a viaduct is necessary to cross the road. The viaduct is similar in style to that which crosses Glen Roy just before Laxey Station, and was probably built by the same contractor, Mark Caine of Douglas, in 1898 when the line was extended towards Ramsey.

Minorca was allegedly given its name by a Manx sailor who had taken part in the battle for Minorca in 1756. If this tale is true then it is unusual as the British lost both the battle and the island, which was ruled by the French for the next seven years. Public opinion was hostile and Admiral John Byng, who had ordered the fleet's return to Gibraltar, was court-martialled for dereliction of duty. On 14 March 1757 he was the last British Admiral to be executed by firing squad. 14 May 2012

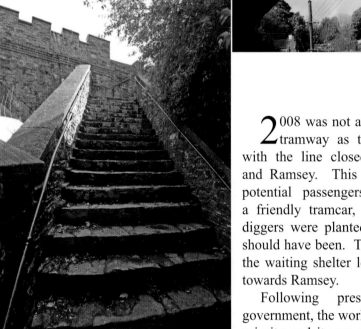

In order to reach the tramway from street level it is necessary to climb these steps from the uphill side of the viaduct. A few more steps at the top will bring intending passengers to the shelter. The elevated position of Minorca guarantees a good view over Laxey Bay and, as the tramway is clearly visible across the valley at South Cape, northbound travellers have about ten minutes warning of the arrival of their tram. 19 May 2009

2008 was not a good year for the tramway as the season started with the line closed between Laxey and Ramsey. This sad sight greeted potential passengers as rather than a friendly tramcar, dump trucks and diggers were planted where the track should have been. This is a view from the waiting shelter looking up the hill towards Ramsey.

Following pressure from the government, the work was given a high priority and it was possible to open a single line from Laxey to Ramsey, with a passing loop at Ballaskeig, before the end of the season. As the northern part of the MER is the more scenic then late season tourists certainly had the better Manx holiday experience.

The line was fully re-opened for the 2009 season but this sad sight serves a reminder of a less than ideal time on the MER. 6 May 2008

Having climbed the main flight of steps up from Minorca Hill, plus the final few from the landing, the waiting shelter is at track level. This shelter originally stood by the line at Halfway, or if you prefer, Baldromma or The Liverpool Arms (see page 30). It is one of the traditional lineside shelters painted in MER green with the nameboard at roof level. 14 May 2012

On a day when the weather is poor then the waiting shelter here presents a welcome: clean, with comfortable seats and with the doorway not facing the prevailing wind. The current MER timetable is displayed on the wall, and occasionally the previous season's timetable as well! 14 May 2012

The photographer was waiting for the first service car when he saw, across the valley, an open motor passing South Cape. He was rewarded when the open motor did not stop at Laxey but continued on up the hill.

Built in 1906, car 33 is powering up the climb towards Ramsey. The livery is unusual having resplendent varnished wood car sides instead of the more usual white paint. Obviously this is not a service car, and 'drying out' runs usually turn at Laxey so why were they here? 12 May 2000

Late in the afternoon blue-and-white liveried car 7 with trailer 46 drifts down to Laxey with a southbound service. The motor car is on the Minorca viaduct, as can be seen from the castellations. Fortunately there was a gap in the foliage of just the right size to be able to see the tram. On the uphill side of the tramway the road bends sharply and climbs very steeply to rejoin the main A2 road at Minorca crossroads at the top of the hill. Please note: the photograph is taken from private property. 12 May 2012

Here we see winter saloon 20 with winter trailer 58 passing Minorca with a northbound service. This is a somewhat unusual combination to be running in normal service on a day in May. The car set will be stabled at Ramsey shed overnight and will form the first service back to Douglas on the next morning. The winter trailers see relatively light use compared with the open trailers and the MER Crest on the dash of the trailer shows that it is a long time since it was last repainted. 17 May 2012 *(Sara Goodwins)*

LAXEY OLD ROAD

The stop at pole 424 is where a steep and stony track crosses the tramway having climbed up from beside the river bridge in old Laxey. The track is a continuation of the Old Laxey Hill which crosses the tramway at Preston's Crossing on the south side of Laxey valley (see page 43). Originally a mediaeval packhorse road known as Puncheon Road, Laxey Old Road was once the only way into old Laxey village from the north and, from the tram stop, continues uphill to cross the main road and join the secondary road through Ballaragh. 'Puncheon' suggests that the road was named after the large cask used for transporting liquor – the name comes from the style of the cask and not its capacity

which was usually between 70 and 120 gallons. The route from Laxey harbour up Laxey Old Road past St Nicholas's Keeill and over Ballaragh would have been very convenient for smugglers, so quite a few puncheons may have passed.

Another suggested derivation of 'Puncheon' is that it is a poor transliteration of *Bayr Unjin*, which is Manx for 'road of the ash tree'. However, photographs of the Laxey valley when the tramway was new show very few trees, so either this was a special tree or this is not the source of the word.

Here car 9 is showing the boards for the 125th anniversary of the Isle of Man Railway from the previous year's celebration. This is an early morning photograph and a motorman experience lesson is under way as the car heads towards Ramsey. 7 May 1999

Winter saloon 19 has rounded the headland above Laxey and is coasting downhill past the stop with a late afternoon service to Douglas. It is only a few minutes since the photographer alighted from a northbound car and just round the corner a crew change has taken place. The same crew returning on a different car are not entirely surprised to find

the passenger that they had recently deposited waiting to take another photograph – hence the friendly wave.

Laxey Old Road is, like many tracks on the island, a right of way for motorcycles, and the steep path emerges very abruptly onto the railway crossing. During 2013 standard road warning signs were installed here. There is little doubt that the motorcycle would come off worse in any collision with a tram. It is hoped that there has not been an unfortunate incident. 8 May 2007

Skinscoe (pole 458) is the first stop on the northern side of the Laxey valley after the tramway has resumed its path parallel to the island's east coast. Skinscoe Farm was once part of the Abbey Lands, an area of land north of Laxey which had been owned by Rushen Abbey. The old bridge down to which Laxey Old Road runs is often called Monks' Bridge, probably because monks built it to access their land to the north.

Skinscoe comes from the Scandinavian *skinskör*. *Skör* means edge or cleft – *cor* is 'edge' in Manx but can only be used for land. Skinscoe or Skynnescor as it used to be known, therefore probably means 'Skinni's Edge' after the owner or occupier who was a skinner.

Here car 5, with an unidentified trailer, is braking to stop at Skinscoe on its way to Douglas with the first service of the day. 9 May 2002

This view shows a crew change taking place, fortuitously at the Skinscoe stop, probably a few hundred yards further along the line than the crew change on page 69. Depending on the timetable, crew changes may or may not be necessary. If, for example, a car makes two-and-a-half return journeys then it will come out of service at the other end of the line from where it entered service in the morning. No problem for the tram, but not so convenient for the crews: how do they get home? Crew changes allow the people concerned to return at the end of their shifts to where they started when their shift began. When a crew change is due, the motormen watch for the approaching car on the other line and then stop appropriately. The changeover takes place where the two trams converge whether it's at a recognised stop or not. Crews may get off but passengers must keep their seats unless at an official halt.

No extra time is built into the timetable for the change, so crews collect their gear, pass the time of day, notify their opposite numbers about helpful information, such as whether passengers wish to alight at unusual stops, and then take the new car back the way they came.

The photographer is on open trailer 46 hauled by car 6 and thankfully the traction pole is not obscuring the action. Under new management winter saloon 22 and trailer 44 will continue north to Ramsey for overnight stabling, while 6 and 46 return to base at Douglas. 9 May 2007

It is late in the season so car 6 is running single motor; what steam enthusiasts would know as light engine. It has climbed from Laxey and rounded the curve to draw up to Skinscoe. Further climbing is still necessary beyond here as the line continues its ascent to the north.

Please note: Skinscoe is one of the stops on the MER designed to serve the farms through which it runs. There is no public access to the stop, apart from by tramway. 5 October 2013

BALLAMOAR BOTTOM

The Ballamoar Bottom stop is located a mere 4 poles north of Skinscoe, at pole 462. Ballamoar, or more correctly Ballamooar means 'big farm' in Manx. Not surprisingly there are a number of other Ballamooars around the island. This one must have been a particularly large farm as it has two stops on the MER, although they are mere three poles apart.

A possible explanation for the two stops is that the farm was made up of two separate areas of land (quarterlands) and rented by two different tenant farmers. Farms in the Isle of Man are traditionally formed out of quarterlands, four of which form one treen. Consequently, although the whole may have belonged to one owner and been a single large agricultural unit, there may have been two establishments both of which the MER chose to serve. This is supposition, but such an agricultural arrangement happens elsewhere on Mann, so is logically possible.

On this stretch of the line, between Skinscoe and Ballaragh, one of the hazards that the motormen expect is the herd of wild goats which roam freely in the fields – and over the fences. The flock may look as though they are farmed but this is not so. As there is no winter service the return of the tram service in the spring tends to disrupt the herd's freedom to roam. Many passengers experience an unexpected braking of the cars in this area and the avoidance of goats on the track is the most likely cause.

In a stretch of line with few landmarks the most distinguishing feature of the stop is the feeder box by the pole. 5 October 2013

BALLAMOAR TOP

Ballamoar Top is located at pole 465. The signwriting is not up the usual high standards of the MER (!) but we can see from the two small photographs that the stop is recognised. Facilities are basic; in the rain the rare passengers huddle under a bush! There is a long straight run here as the line steadily gains height heading north. Winter saloon 22 is coasting downhill towards Laxey and the motorman must be wondering if he will need to halt and collect the photographer at this little-used stop. 5 October 2013

Ballaragh (pole 488) is where the MER and the main Douglas to Ramsey, A2, road rejoin each other, the railway having taken a longer and gentler climb than the road. This is another 'farm' name derived from *balla* or *balley*, although there is some uncertainty about what the rest of the name means. It could be a corruption of Ballacarrick – Ballaragh is pronounced, roughly, bal-*ar*-ack – which would mean 'farm of the edge'. This would be appropriate for two reasons. Firstly Ballaragh village is about a quarter of a mile inland from the stop and the area is above the steep cliffs at Bulgham; secondly the area is close to the boundary between the Lonan and Maughold parishes.

There are also some suggestions that the second part of the name is from the Manx *arraght* meaning 'to endure' or *arragh* meaning the season of spring. One of the distinctive green painted MER shelters used to be located here, but this was demolished in 1973.

In this view we see winter saloon 22 carrying a representation of the then Isle of Man transport bus livery approaching with a service for Douglas. 8 May 2002

A few years later and the same winter saloon is seen at almost exactly the same spot as before. It has now reverted to the more traditional livery. The consensus was that the bus-style livery was inappropriate and unattractive on the tram. The crossover has since been relocated to lie a few yards to the south of the stop, rather than the north as seen here. This probably happened during the permanent way works which took place during 2008.

Behind the tram we see that interchange between bus and tram is encouraged as both flags are present on the pole beside the main road behind the wall. The gap in the wall to access the tram stop is a few yards from the bus stop but still convenient. Out of sight on the far side of the road a footpath leads up the hill to Ballaragh village. 13 September 2006

Exactly five years after the last photograph we now see the rebuilt car 7 with trailer 48 in matching blue and white livery starting away from Ballaragh. Northwards from here the road and the railway run very closely together, with the cliff having been cut away to provide a ledge for the two means of transport. The cliff face has been fitted with steel netting secured by rock bolts to restrain falling boulders from landing on the carriageway or bouncing onto the tramway. The sheer drop to the rocks of Bulgham Bay around 500 feet below is impressive.

In the fields between the tram stop and the cliffs passengers can often see a small herd of Manx loaghtan sheep. This rare breed, complete with its splendid sets of horns (four or six per sheep) and distinctive brown fleece is one of the island's most famous animals – along with the Manx cat. 13 September 2011

Looking to the south (and almost directly into the sun) tunnel car 6 and trailer 44 are departing from Ballaragh. The relocated crossover is visible shortly in front of the tram. From here it is downhill all the way to Laxey. 25 August 2013

BULGHAM

Is Bulgham (pole 507) a stop or not? If a conductor is asked for Bulgham they will not stop the car here. Yet there is a platform with a signwritten MER name which looks like it should be a stop but which has no public access to or from the adjacent road. In fact this is a viewing platform added to the MER in 2009, and with its first recorded use in August of that year. Normal service cars do not call here. Only special cars or arranged tours will stop so that the participants can descend and enjoy the view from the cliffs, before reboarding and continuing southwards. On balance the presence of the sign swung the argument that this is a stop of sorts and hence worthy of inclusion.

There is disagreement about the derivation of the name Bulgham. *Bolgum*, itself a corruption of *Beeal-gym*, means an opening with liquid in it; *beeal* meaning mouth, entrance or passageway, and *gym* meaning liquid. The alternative is that *bolg* in Manx means a belly, while the -an suffix indicates a dimunitive, hence 'little belly'. There is also the

suggestion that *bolg* could mean a windy place.

In January 1940 during a snowstorm with a strong onshore wind, the Fleetwood trawler *Merissa* ran aground on the rocks in Bulgham Bay. Despite the efforts of the Ramsey lifeboat and rocket brigade all twelve crew drowned. At very low tide parts of the wreck can sometimes be seen from passing MER cars.

Here winter saloon 20 with closed trailer 58 passes with a southbound service. 18 May 2012

Now you see it, now you don't! Looking down from the top of the cliffs we can see southbound car 5 and trailer 40 at the site of what is now the Bulgham viewing platform. This was also before the renewal and extension of steel netting undertaken early in the twenty-first century to prevent loose boulders falling onto the road and tramway; the cliffs in the foreground are now covered with steel netting.

The stretch of line cut into the cliffs of Bulgham has presented the MER with considerable difficulties over the years. The most significant problem was in 1967. In mid-afternoon on 20 January 1967 a masonry wall supporting

the line where it crosses a cleft in the cliff collapsed. The tram service was maintained on either side of the break, with passengers walking between two temporary stations on either side of the rupture.

Fortunately, the Manx government funded the repairs needed or this could have meant the end of services between Ramsey and Laxey. Major strengthening of the track support was required and after a concentrated effort the line was finally re-opened to through traffic on 10 July 1967, mid-way through the summer season. 7 May 2004

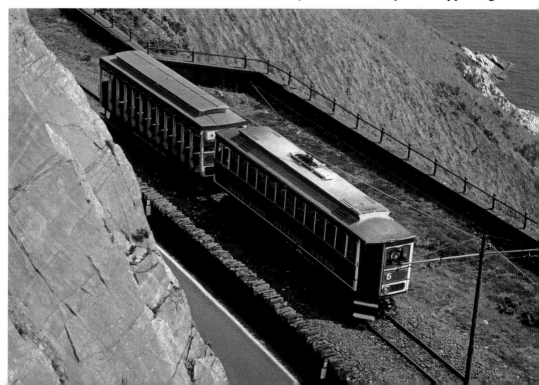

DHOON GLEN

Dhoon Glen (pole 531) is situated where the old road from Laxey via Ballaragh village joins the main (A2) coast road, at the bottom of a slight drop from the summit at Bulgham. The name appears to come from the Manx *doon* meaning to shut up or darken – appropriate as the glen is very narrow and steep-sided and contains the island's longest waterfall. This derivation is apparently wrong, however!

Most authorities agree that the word comes from the Manx for 'fort', also *doon*, even though the word is rarely used with that meaning in Manx. Across the road from the tramway there is a mound of earth with steep sides, just like a fort.

Even that is not so simple as the two words spring from the same root. *Doon* originally meant a fence or enclosure. In Ireland the word moved to mean the fort (i.e., the thing enclosed) while on the Isle of Man it retained the meaning of shutting up, but with the added feeling of darkening; the glen can be a gloomy place under the trees.

Here winter saloon 22 and trailer 43 pause at Dhoon Glen with a southbound service, with a waiting passenger ready to board. 9 May 2000

Dhoon Glen boasts above average facilities compared with many stops along the line. In addition to the wooden waiting hut there are toilets and a café, seen here behind the shelter, with outside tables for a fine day. For some years the café traded under the name 'Jean's Place' and was later known as 'Harry's Halt'. It is open most days when the trams are running and many weekends in the winter when they are not.

The glen leads down to the beach and there are two alternative paths from the station area – one descends the glen rather precipitously past the waterfall and the other drops more gently over the southern shoulder. This latter gives good views back towards the cliffs and the tramway at Bulgham and Ballaragh.

On the other side of the main road the car park was once the site of the Dhoon Glen Hotel, built in 1886. The next year, considered to be poor from the weather point of view, it catered for 42,000 visitors. Unfortunately the hotel was destroyed by fire in 1932; the remains of its lower walls may be seen at the back of the car park. 13 May 2012

Drawing into Dhoon Glen with a service for Ramsey is the blue and white liveried car 7 with trailer 48. Reflected in the motorman's windscreen are the twin flags on the pole behind the photographer showing that it is possible to catch either the main road bus or the tram from this point. Also visible through the windscreen is the electric bell behind the motorman's shoulder; this is the rebuilt car 7 and the modern feature has replaced the previous rod operated bell.

Unusually the Dhoon Glen stop is situated on a sharp curve, which is particularly evident in the abrupt change in direction that the overhead wire takes here. The sight lines for the conductor are difficult for northbound cars.

The rails are glistening: evidently there has been a shower and the photographer has listened for the sound of the approaching tram before deserting the shelter and crossing the line. 18 May 2012

Having descended from the summit at Bulgham the tramway now runs through predominantly rural farming country most of it in the parish of Maughold. After the sharp turn at Dhoon Glen the first halt is Burn's Crossing at pole 540.

Burn is this instance is not a person's name but comes from the Scots for stream. Dhoon Glen is fed by several streams flowing down from Glen Callin ('Callin's glen'), Glion Lomarcan ('glen on its own') and Glion yn Ard ('glen on the height'). Burn's Crossing is near where one of the streams crosses beneath the MER tracks on its tumbling way down to Dhoon Glen and the sea.

The main Douglas to Ramsey A2 coast road lies behind the trees on the right of this view of winter saloon 20 and trailer 46 heading the first northbound service of the day. There is no doubt about the location with the pole number and stop flag both clearly visible. 13 May 2012 *(Sara Goodwins)*

Tunnel car 9 and trailer 43 head south at Burn's Crossing with a morning service from Ramsey to Douglas. The stop is reached by a short path down from the A2 road. Sandwiched between the main road and the tramway is a cottage with a private gateway at the corner of the path and the tramway giving convenient access to the stop which lies near the back door.

In the background can be seen the workings of Dhoon Quarry (see page 80) which is carved out of the hill to the east of the tramway. The quarry was owned by the Isle of Man Highways Board and stone was carried by a ropeway to the tramway for transportation, often to the island's capital. The quarry produced granite setts which were used, among other things, to pave the streets along the line of the Upper Douglas cable tramway. 13 May 2012

The tramway runs close to the main Douglas to Ramsey road and the next stop at Dhoon Farm (pole 550) is also reached by a short footpath, in this case connecting the main road with the lane which crossed the tramway at the Dhoon Glen stop.

Here winter saloon 21 and trailer 40 are viewed from the steep path which crosses the line by the stop. The car set is on a southbound service to Douglas and has just climbed up from Dhoon Quarry. 20 May 2010

As it is winter there is no tram service today. Looking towards Dhoon Glen, the farm which the stop serves is on the right, sandwiched between the tramway and the main road. Traction pole 550 has been replaced recently and the stop flag has presumably remained with the prevous pole.

The semi-circular wall on the right is a remnant of a Nissen hut type structure. Such huts were used in their thousands during both world wars as cheap prefabricated buildings. The corrugated iron skin has probably rusted away but the concrete end supports still stand as a reminder. 2 February 2014

The tramway served two quarries at the Dhoon Quarry stop (pole 556). The first of these is Dhoon Quarry itself, already seen in the background from Burn's Crossing (see page 78). A number of sidings were installed on the east or sea side of the tramway to provide wagon storage and loading facilities. The site of these is clearly visible and the level space is now often used to store permanent way materials such as new rails, sleepers and ballast.

A second quarry, Dhoon West Quarry, was situated to the west of the line, beyond the main coast road. Dhoon West was owned by the MER and connected to it by a 2'-0" gauge tramway which passed beneath the road in a tunnel. The tramway approached almost at right angles to the loading dock which is still visible with its own siding set off from the northbound MER line. The bay is still used to load ballast into hopper wagons for permanent way works, but the stone is no longer quarried locally. Both quarries produced granite setts, and the export market for these was also a factor in justifying the economics of the extension of the tramway to Ramsey.

In this view tunnel car 7, which at the time was the usual choice for works duties, is seen waiting on the northbound line with the trolley turned ready to follow the southbound service car from which the photograph was taken. A flat car loaded with rails is attached behind car 7, so presumably these are destined for the next re-laying project. The loading bay is on the siding to the left of the car. Unusually for a tramway there used to be a weighbridge in this siding; it was used for weighing outgoing quarry products. 10 May 2001

Crossing the the lane from Dhoon Glen, winter saloon 21 and trailer 40 form a southbound service passing Dhoon Quarry. On the extreme right of the picture the line to Ramsey can be seen climbing away from the quarry loading area. Dhoon Quarry gives an unusually industrial appearance to the line in what is mainly a rural area. 20 May 2010 *(Sara Goodwins)*

Car 6 is approaching the stop at Dhoon Quarry with a southbound service. To the right of the car is the area where stone was transferred from the aerial ropeway to the MER wagons. The sidings have been removed but a quantity of ballast is visible with more modern loading equipment. In the siding which remains on the other side of the line is a ballast hopper wagon. This is approximately where the weighbridge used to be when freight traffic generated profits for the MER. The loading bay for Dhoon West Quarry lies behind the ballast hopper. 4 May 2004

A close up of the ballast hopper in the siding shows several interesting features. No number is visible, but it is vehicle 21 in the list of freight rolling stock. It was adapted to a ballast wagon from a flat-bed truck, probably in summer 2000; eighteen months later the height of the hoppers was increased. The stated capacity is 6 tons which means that the loaded wagon is likely to be heavier than a standard trailer with 48 seats. However when a power car is hauling the hopper wagon it will not also have a full load inside so an unladen power car plus laden ballast wagon will weigh much the same as a laden power car plus laden trailer. The power requirements will therefore be similar. On wet or greasy rails, lack of adhesion with the power car may however make uphill sections heavier going. The ballast wagon also has heavier duty bogies than are found on some of the trailers.

The wagon is unloaded by opening the bottom doors allowing emerging ballast to be directed to either the centre of the track or the ballast shoulders to either side. Much of the MER is built on a rocky foundation with few areas of soft ground. A permanent-way engineer's dream. 8 May 2007

This view is taken through the rear window of a northbound trailer. In the siding is tunnel car 9 – confirmed by the evidence of the additional lights – which is attached to the permanent way flat car 45. On the left of the running lines beyond the tunnel car can be seen a stockpile of new rails. Beyond car 9 the siding used to join the northbound running line near the stop, but this connexion has since been removed. The small tramway which connected with Dhoon West Quarry passed the far side of the small building – it used to be a smithy – on the other side of the road on the right in this view and terminated near this siding.

In a few minutes the next car to pass Dhoon Quarry will be the first southbound car of the day, after which car 9 and flat 45 will have a window to work on the line. 12 May 2007

Thalloo Mitchell (pole 563) is located just north of the Dhoon Quarry sidings area. The name is usually understood to mean 'Michael's ground'; *thalloo* means a small plot of land. In mediaeval times Thalloo Vitchell was part of the lands owned by Rushen Abbey and offered hospitality to travellers. In Manx the first letter of words beginning in M can mutate to V in some grammatical constructs. A separate building acted as something like a hostel for the homeless.

However there is some thought that the area was known as Tholt y Mitchell. If so, it means Michael's tholtan, or ruined farm buildings. Mitchell may be the English surname rather than the name Michael. Some argue that 'Tholt y' was replaced by 'Thalloo' because of the proximity of Thalloo Queen (see Brown's Crossing on the next page).

Here we see winter saloon 20 approaching with a Douglas bound service. In the left background can be seen the lane which passes by the landward side of the sidings at Dhoon Quarry and its junction with the main road between Douglas and Ramsey. 9 May 2001

Thalloo Mitchell is on the treen known as the Particles. In the fifteenth century this land was divided into 'particles' for the support of scholars so that they could concentrate on teaching. The support thus provided acted as an early form of academic tenure.

When the MER was built the Corlett family lived at Thalloo Mitchell. Different members of the family worked as farmers and miners and at least one was a joiner.

Here we see winter saloon 21 and trailer 47 departing for Ramsey. Above the bank separating the track from the road can be seen the road crossing signs and the stop flag for Brown's Crossing just a few poles further north. 16 May 2010

BROWN'S CROSSING

Brown's Crossing (pole 568) is a mere five poles further along the line from Thalloo Mitchell. The crossing was almost certainly named after an individual. Brown is a well-respected Manx surname, the Manx national poet is T.E. Brown and in Laxey, Brown's Café (see page 64) has also been well known to generations of visitors. It would seem logical that the crossing should be named after the occupant of the house next to it but nothing has (yet) been found to confirm this.

The road which leaves the A2 and crosses the tramway here descends to Thalloo Queen farm and ultimately to Port Cornaa. In this view winter saloon 20 and trailer 46 head south. The shutters on the trailer are nearly all pulled down to protect the interior from the inclement weather. 9 May 2007

Travelling in the opposite direction tunnel car 6 with an unidentified trailer have arrived at Brown's Crossing with a service for Ramsey. The motorman has stopped across the highway and is waiting for the photographer's southbound car and trailer to pass before resuming his journey; the conductor would otherwise be at his station on the back platform.

One interesting feature of MER operations is that when two cars pass each other in the vicinity of a road crossing, the first car to arrive will stop across the highway and wait for the second car to pass it: the two cars will then pull away and clear the crossing virtually simultaneously. This is a safety procedure and ensures that road users cannot assume that the first car is the only one and drive into the second as it emerges behind the first on the further track. 21 May 2009

BALLELIN

From Brown's Crossing the MER follows the main Douglas to Ramsey road, usually running slightly below the road, until near the Glen Mona stop.

Ballelin (pole 579) is named after the farm which it serves. Another *balla* word but contracted. It means 'Allen's Farm' and a family called Allen were recorded as living here in the sixteenth century. The surname might have derived from *alainn* (Scottish Gaelic) or *alaind* (Erse), both of which mean beautiful. On the other hand, Allen was the surname of several vicars of Maughold, the first of whom is said to have originated in Norfolk – not a Gaelic-speaking area. Allen and its derivatives are not common Manx surnames and the family name has long gone; the Quayle family have been farming here for over a hundred years.

At the beginning of the fourteenth century the farm was the cause of a dispute between the Abbot of Rushen Abbey and the Prior of St Bees in Cumbria. Both claimed that their monastic orders had been given the farm by Alexander III of Scotland who ruled Mann at that time. Edward of England eventually settled that the Prior got Ballelin (but see Ballajora, page 113) and the Abbott received Dhoon Glen, which was also under dispute.

Here we see tunnel car 9 with almost invisible trailer 47 operating a southbound service. 20 May 2010

Treens were generally divided into four quarterlands – hence, obviously, the name – and the usual pattern was that each quarterland made up a farm. The Ballig quarterland is unusual as it seems to be the only one in the Rencullen treen. It is not clear why there are the two names, and indeed Ballig was known as Rencullen at the end of the eighteenth century. Ballig means 'farm of the hollow' and there are several farms of this name on Mann. The name derives from *balla*, 'farm', and *lagg*, 'hollow'. In the late nineteenth century the farm was inhabited by the Kneen family, some of whom also lived at Thalloo Mitchell (see page 83).

The stop is at pole 590 and a couple of passengers are boarding Ramsey-bound car 20, preferring the comforts of the winter saloon to those of trailer 44. The conductor has descended to the lineside to offer assistance if necessary. In the background, on a bend in the tramway and the main road, is a house which looks as though it would be rather more at home in suburban London than the Manx countryside. 12 May 2007

This day was the 120th anniversary of the opening of the MER and a special high frequency service was operating. Unfortunately the weather was atrocious and here we see winter saloon 22 heading north at Ballig in the rain. There is no trailer attached as the car will collect a mailvan from Ramsey and re-enact the once common sight of an MER tram with van attached, on its return journey to Douglas later in the afternoon.

Winter saloon 22 is one of the trams fitted with an additional high-intensity headlight which can be seen mounted below the dash on the car's nearside. The MER operates relatively few services during the hours of darkness but these lights, which unlike the main headlight, are not in circuit with the traction current, assist at these times. 7 September 2013

Around the corner from Ballig lies Ballasholague at pole 602. Alternative spellings are Ballashaughlaig and Ballashellag. Once again *balla* means 'farm' while the original *sheillagh* means 'black willow'. Cregeen's dictionary is definite about the meaning of *sheillagh* being 'salix, black willows or sally'. The genus *salix* covers around 400 species of willow, but 'black willow' is native to North America, indicating that this is not a native plant. Once the plant was introduced, the Manx had to call it something however, and, according to Cregeen, *sheillagh* was it.

Seen from the front passenger seat of southbound winter saloon 19 we see car 9 heading north having just passed the stop flag at Ballasholague. The Douglas to Ramsey main road is on the right of the line behind the hedgerow and the stop is accessed from the road. The handbrake handle of car 19 is visible in the bottom right of the photograph. The handbrake is not normally used in service but acts as a parking brake and can be held on by a ratchet. It is, of course, available for emergency use. 13 September 2011

Ballasholague Farm has the dubious distinction of being one of two farms which introduced foot-and-mouth disease to the island in 1882. The farm's then owner, Andrew Milligan of Dromore in Scotland, had purchased eighteen head of cattle and imported them on the schooner *The Three Brothers*. He was a noted cattle doctor, and although he might have been expected to notice that the beasts were ill before bringing them to the island, he did at least arrange for them to be quarantined in Ramsey. Six days later they were released and brought to Ballasholague. Sadly this proved premature. The disease raged for several months before being eradicated in February 1883. The island has had no further outbreak since. During the major UK outbreak in 2001, strong measures, including cancelling the TT races, were implemented to protect the island's herds.

Here we see tunnel car 9 again forming a northbound service and approaching the Ballasholague stop. 14 September 2011

Despite appearances, this is not a crew change (see page 71). During the early part of the 2012 season there was single line working beyond Lewaigue (see page 119) because of an earth slip onto the MER tracks at Windy Ridge between Bellevue and Ballure (see pages 122 and 125). Structural engineers had to encroach onto the MER tracks to clear the fall and stabilise the bank. The line further from the sea was closed while the work was underway, opening later in May. During the single-line working the MER introduced a staff and ticket operation. Here the conductor of car 20 with trailer 46, the first Douglas-bound car of the day, has paused to pass the staff to his opposite number on car 7 and 48. Coincidentally the exchange took place at Corkhill's Crossing (pole 607).

During 2013, single-line working was back in operation with, this time, the line nearer to the sea closed. Essential cliff stabilisation work began and, although not encroaching directly onto the MER track, it was considered safer to close the line nearer the sea to allow for a safety margin between heavy earth moving vehicles and the passing MER rolling stock. During the busy peak season both lines were open; either the cliff work was suspended or extra care was taken.

This stop was previously known as Looney's Crossing. Cork(h)ill and Looney are both old Manx names of families who have lived for many generations in Maughold, and indicate that the stop is named after an individual or family and not a farm. 15 May 2012 *(Sara Goodwins)*

Corkhill is generally thought to be contracted from something like *Mac-þór-Ketill* which means, literally, the son or family of Thor's kettle/cauldron. The story of Thor's cauldron was a favourite Norse saga of traditional length and complex genealogy. Suffice it to say that the cauldron was taken by Thor from the giant Hymir as it was the only container large enough to brew mead for all the gods. The forename Torquil comes from the same root.

The stop's old name of Looney's Crossing comes from the Irish name O'Luinigh which in turn comes from *luinneach* meaning 'bearing arms'.

The house by the crossing, just out of view to the right, is prominently named 'Barony View', because the hill to the south east and seaward is Barony Hill. All the barony lands on the island were owned by ecclesiastical barons, i.e., the church, and Barony Hill was once owned by St Bees Priory in Cumberland. On a brilliant October day we see winter saloon 21 heading single motor towards Douglas. The road behind the tram heads up a short rise to Glen Mona and the only remaining inn between Laxey and Ramsey, the Glen Mona Hotel. 5 October 2013

The Manx Heritage Transport Festival in 2013 took place over the five-day period between 24 and 28 July. This featured special events on the island railways and the MER was, of course, included. On 28 July a high-frequency service was operated which required practically all serviceable cars to be running, and required a major effort from the staff of the tramway to ensure both car and crew availability. Fortunately the weather obliged with a warm sunny day which made the task of crewing the open fronted cars more pleasureable than it would otherwise have been. With a fifteen-minute service interval the opportunities to ride on the trams and photograph them were excellent.

Here we see open motor car 16 with trailer 60 approaching Glen Mona and emerging from the shade under the trees to draw up at the stop. This pair of cars is painted in the livery introduced in 1957 after the MER was nationalized and discontinued shortly thereafter. At the time of writing, 16+60 are the only cars to bear this colour scheme. 28 July 2013

Also seen at Glen Mona on the same day is the combination of motor car 1 and trailer 51, both of which were present at the opening of the original line in 1893. Here a rear view of the lightweight trailer shows that not all the side verticals extend to the roof-line and that there are no shutters on the original trailers. Very refreshing on a sunny day but negligible protection against wind and rain on other days. The cars are heading back to Douglas, having loaded at the stop.

For a period in the late twentieth century trailer 51 reverted to its original number of 13. The inscription 'Douglas & Laxey Coast Electric Tramway' on both cars is sympathetic to the Victorian image presented. 28 July 2013

The stop at Glen Mona (pole 611) is only a field away from the centre of the village of Glen Mona, with the Glen Mona Hotel a short distance up a steep pathway on the inland side of the line.

Glen Mona is the modern name for Glion Shuin. Mona is often used as a soubriquet for the Isle of Man, so the name could be translated as 'Manx glen' which is rather vague, given the number of glens on the island. Glen Shuin, which is what the glen was called until the mid-nineteenth century, means 'rush glen'.

Between 1854 and 1857 and again from 1866 to 1867 Glen Mona was home to the Great Mona Mining Company, which may be why the Glen was rechristened at about this time. The company sank a lead mine to fifty fathoms (100 yards) but produced little of value and the workings were discontinued.

Here we see a southbound service formed of winter saloon 20 with an unidentified trailer about to call at the stop. 11 May 2001

Glen Mona, being where a relatively large number of passengers board, warrants the first waiting shelter on the line since Dhoon Glen (see page 80). In this instance a wooden shelter is provided rather than one of the traditional green-painted corrugated iron type. Over the years the trees have grown up around the line here and the shelter is now almost shrouded by the canopy. The path from the village descends on the other side of the line from the shelter.

Prior to the abandonment of mail collection by the MER in 1975 one of the brick built post boxes stood here, but as there is no direct road access for collection by van, the post box has now disappeared. Note the bicycle. The MER will carry bicycles, particularly on the trailers if there is room, but passengers come first, probably because they are paying! 28 July 2013

The glen has obviously been associated with the supernatural, to judge from the names given to the natural features to be found in it. A hole in the rock of the river is called Cass y Foawr ('foot of the giant') from its shape. The same giant presumably threw Creg y Foawr ('rock of the giant') into the glen. In the stream, which runs parallel to the path down from the village past the stop and on to the sea at Port Cornaa, is Lhing y Glashtin ('pool of the sprite or goblin').

Back in the real world, tunnel car 9 and trailer 46 form a southbound service to Douglas and the motorman is drawing to a halt by the shelter. 17 May 2009

According to Cregeen's dictionary a *garey* is a garden. The meaning of *garee* is however a 'sour piece of land', which, as this stop adjoins a sewage works, could perhaps be more appropriate.

The Garey (pole 616) was once called Dhoon Church, and the church is visible across the field towards the main road. Built in 1855 as a chapel of ease for Kirk Maughold it replaced the original Dhoon Church which was built at Dhoon Bridge about a mile to the south – which is why Dhoon Church is in Glen Mona and not Dhoon. It seems the church was originally dedicated to the Holy Trinity but is now Christchurch. If the church looks similar to that by Laxey Station this is not surprising as the same architect, Ewan Christian, designed both. His most famous work on the island is probably St Thomas's church in Douglas.

Here we see winter saloon 20, complete with vinyl covered dash celebrating 120 years of the MER, approaching the dip by the stop, with a southbound service, a couple of weeks before the end of the 2013 season. 15 October 2013

A road leads down to the stop from the main road through Glen Mona, makes an abrupt turn immediately before the tracks are reached and then turns again to cross the line by the stop. The lane provides access to the local sewage plant, which has recently been modernized, and then becomes a private road leading to Ballagorry Farm. Where the road bends at the bottom of the drop a steel crash barrier has been installed – hopefully this does not reflect an unfortunate incident in the past.

Although this stop is at the approach to Ballagorry Farm it is the stop after this one which bears the Ballagorry name. Northbound winter saloon 21, with no trailer, slows and will shortly continue its journey to Ramsey. 15 October 2013

In the section on Glen Mona (see page 89) we saw open motor 16 and trailer 60 travelling towards Douglas. Earlier in the afternoon the duo had made an outward journey to Ramsey and here they are climbing up from The Garey towards Ballagorry on the northbound line.

For many years the two farms Ballagorry Mooar and Ballagorry Beg (big and little respectively) were farmed by the Corkhill family, presumably the same as gave their name to the crossing three stops earlier. 28 July 2013

From the low spot of The Garey the line rises slightly to Ballagorry stop at pole 624. The name means 'Gorry's Farm' but there never seems to have been a Gorry family who lived here. There are a couple of possibilities. Gorry, or Gorree is the Manx form of Godred, and Godred Crovan is an important figure in Manx history credited with introducing Tynwald. Perhaps a farmer in antiquity wanted to aggrandise his farm, rather as builders name roads 'King's Drive' and the like. As an alternative, the word may be a corruption of *garey* or *goree*, as detailed for the previous stop.

The stop at The Garey can be seen at the bottom of the dip behind winter saloon 21 and trailer 40 as they climb to Ballagorry from the south. 20 May 2010

Winter saloon 22 and trailer 40 have just passed Ballagorry heading north. They are dropping to pass beneath Ballagorry bridge, the only overbridge on the MER, which can be seen in the background.

The bridge was constructed in 1901 by Joshua Shaw, engineer and secretary of the company that owned the MER. The bridge was built to provide field access for a local farmer; presumably the line had severed his land and the cutting prevented easy access to part of the farm.

Originally constructed of wood, the bridge was rebuilt in the 1950s of reinforced concrete faced with stone. In 1989 the power supply to this section of line was updated and a substation was incorporated below the deck of the overbridge in its eastern parapet.

The change of gradient at the rail ends is accentuated in this photograph by the telephoto lens and is not nearly as abrupt as it may appear! 28 July 2013

A power feed is provided at the pole nearest to the bridge and it is good practice to shut off power and coast beneath such section breaks. Unusually this is on an uphill gradient of 1 in 24. Coasting uphill tests the skills and judgement of even the most experienced motormen. Here we see tunnel car 9 with trailer 47 approaching from the north. 20 May 2010

WATSON'S CROSSING

Winter saloon 22 just after it passed Watson's Crossing, well lit in bright sunshine. On the ground between the tracks in front of the car is part of a dead traction pole awaiting removal. Replacing rusted or damaged poles is a very important part of keeping the tramway running and, with nearly 1,000 poles to maintain, requires considerable forward planning. Each traction pole can be expected to last at least twenty years, although some, notably those inherited from the Douglas Head Marine Drive Tramway (see page 114), have lasted very much longer. 5 October 2013

Watson's Crossing (pole 636) is at the lower (northern) end of the cutting beyond the Ballagorry Bridge. Unusually, rather than the name being associated with one of the local farms, it is, according to his nephew, named after someone who used to work for the MER. Mr Watson worked at the power station below the line between Dolland and Ballaglass (see next page). Watson's Crossing marks the point where he crossed the line on his way to work every day, using the footpath down into the valley.

Here we see tunnel car 9, with its original illumination scheme using lightbulbs, climbing past Watson's Crossing on a southbound service with trailer 42 in tow. The lights are not powered, but the sunlight has caught them to give an unusual effect. The picture was taken from the back seat of a northbound trailer and is not the result of meticulous planning! 12 May 1998

As is the case with several MER stops, there is no road access to Watson's Crossing. The public access to the stop is about a quarter of a mile's walk along a footpath which leaves the main Douglas to Ramsey road on the steep hill between Glen Mona and Corrany Village.

Here we see that the MER is extremely convenient for these two passengers as winter saloon 22 and trailer 41 have halted to drop them at their gate. You can't get better than that! 18 May 2009

Although winter saloon 20 and trailer 44 have not yet reached Watson's Crossing – that is off to the right – the picture shows clearly the buildings which used to be Ballaglass power station, at which Mr Watson worked. The station ceased to supply the line after August 1934 with the plant being dismantled in 1935. The old power station buildings are now a private residence (see also page 98). 6 May 2007

Another crew change fortuitously taking place at one of the official stops; the Watson's Crossing flag is just visible to the left of the picture. Winter saloon 19 and an unidentified trailer will soon continue on their way to Ramsey, while sister vehicle 21 and 47 head for Douglas. 16 September 2011

Taken on the same occasion as car 22 on page 94, the next southbound car was also well lit – note that the motorman is standing up to avoid being dazzled by the sun. 5 October 2013

Dolland Halt (pole 644) was originally located to serve the cluster of (now ruined) buildings huddled beside the MER tracks. Farming, fishing and mining were the chief sources of income and families usually did a little of each. Life in the island has always been precarious and many Manx families were forced to emigrate to seek greater fortune elsewhere. America was a popular destination and a run of bad harvests between 1825 and 1837 prompted an exodus. The early twentieth century also saw much emigration. Many small farms or crofts were left to become ruins and those at Dolland are by no means rare.

Here we see the photographic charter which we saw earlier in the day at South Cape (see page 45). The rain has abated and the motorman is no longer getting drenched. Having completed a trip to Ramsey, one of the original motor cars of 1893, car 2, leads winter trailer 57 up the slope from Ballaglass past Dolland as it heads back towards Douglas. 6 May 2004

Under trees on the opposite side of the line from the power station, is an example of the sort of ruined farmstead known as a *tholtan* in Manx; this one may be glimpsed from the passing trams. The footpath which crosses the line passes the remains of the cottages and was presumably once the pedestrian access for the families who lived there. 20 May 2010

The surname Dolland is very rare, not only on Mann but generally, and is thought to be a corruption of the Irish Dulin. There is a tiny village in South Dakota called Doland which was founded by emigrants from Britain and Ireland. Until Webster – he of the American dictionary – 'regularized' the spelling it was spelt with two 'L's. Is there a connexion with the Dollands of the Isle of Man?

Dolland is another stop which is accessible only by footpath or tram and the path from Corrany that leads to Watson's Crossing crosses the line here and continues towards Ballaglass Glen down the hill. Here we see winter saloon 21 and trailer 47 climbing up from Ballaglass with a service for Douglas. 16 September 2011

Between the stops at Dolland and Ballaglass Glen the former MER power station is visible below the line (see page 96). When the line was constructed the railway generated all its own electricity as the technology of the day made transmission of power over long distances impractical. The Ballaglass power station supplied the northern section when the tramway was extended from Laxey to Ramsey. It was eventually supplanted by the advent of high tension AC feeders from the Manx Electricty Board the current from which was transformed at substations along the line.

This photograph was taken on the day of the 120th anniversary of the opening of the MER. Still going strong is original 1893 motor car, number 1, matched with trailer 51 of the same vintage. Sadly the day is rainy but the intensive service being operated means that the photographer will not need to wait too long for his next ride in the dry. The cars are heading downhill here towards Ballaglass Glen. 7 September 2013

Note the rain on the lens of the camera! Once again we must salute the motorman for his devotion to duty. Still on the high intensity service for the 120th anniversary we see open motor car 16 and trailer 60 climbing up from Ballaglass. As Dolland is nowhere near any habitable buildings the motorman is surprised to find a passenger waiting here in the rain.

The historic green livery is that of the newly nationalized MER from 1957. 7 September 2013

Car 9 presents a splendid show of light as it swings round the curves towards Ballaglass halt. This car appeared earlier in the day at Laxey Old Road (see page 69) and is operating one of the driver experience sessions. The instructor on this occasion is MER veteran John Matthews, for many years yardmaster and chief motorman, and generally responsible for driver training. The car has been to Ramsey and is now returning to Douglas. Car 9 still displays the illuminated boards for the previous year's Steam 125 celebration.

Ballaglass Glen has some delightful walks and waterfalls. A short descent from the stop brings the walker to the base of the rock embankment which takes the tramway over the stream which flows through Corrany and Ballaglass Glen and eventually joins the sea at Port Cornaa. The large embankment is not immediately obvious from track level but is a major piece of civil engineering. Note: the leaning pole really did lean this much but has since been replaced (see next page). 7 May 1999

Tunnel car 9, with trailer 43 in tow, again approaches Ballaglass, this time with a southbound service car. The illuminations have now been completely re-organized and on not such a gloomy day are switched off.

Compared with the photograph on the previous page we can see that the leaning traction pole has been felled and new pole planted in its place. Maintenance of the poles along the line is a continual task and the identification of corroded poles before they fall and bring the wires down is essential. The previous pole had been clamped at the base where corrosion tends to be worst and filled with concrete as a strengthener, but eventually it had to go. The new pole here is one of the stronger fabricated poles which are used on sharp curves. 13 May 2012

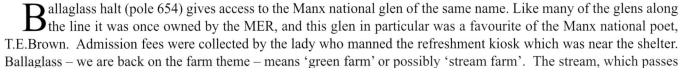

Ballaglass halt (pole 654) gives access to the Manx national glen of the same name. Like many of the glens along the line it was once owned by the MER, and this glen in particular was a favourite of the Manx national poet, T.E.Brown. Admission fees were collected by the lady who manned the refreshment kiosk which was near the shelter. Ballaglass – we are back on the farm theme – means 'green farm' or possibly 'stream farm'. The stream, which passes under the line shortly after the stop, used to turn a wheel for the Ballaglass lead mine. This was a mid-nineteenth century enterprise, another of the not very successful enterprises of the Great Mona Mining Company (see Glen Mona page 90). The two glens are actually very close together, one on each side of the hill topped by Cashtal yn Ard, and meet at Port Cornaa.

The wooden shelter – the picture to the left is a back view of the shelter from the footpath which runs behind it – is unique in that it has a gate. The objective is to dissuade sheltering animals who do not provide custom to the tramway and leave unwelcome calling cards. 13 May 2012

The penultimate day of the 2013 season saw a special photographic event on the MER. The weather did not oblige but the photographer used the Ballaglass shelter as a bolt hole for his early morning shots. Here 'car 3', with royal trailer 59 in tow, heads for Ramsey.

The real car 3, built in 1893, was one of those destroyed in the Laxey car shed fire of 1930. The number on the side of the body gives away the fact that this is car 2 masquerading as its sister car for the event. The change of identity can be effected very rapidly as a fridge-magnet style '3' is deployed to hide the real number. The royal trailer's lights are connected to the power car's circuits and the effect is very inviting.

Trailer 59 is known as the royal trailer because on 25 August 1902 their majesties King Edward VII and Queen Alexandra travelled by MER from Douglas to Ramsey in this trailer. Originally built as a directors' saloon it is

delightful inside but has a very peculiar yawing motion when being towed owing to the fact that it is very short and the bogies are very close together. The royal family regularly travel by train but rarely by tram. Undoubtedly the MER was proud of upstaging the steam railway which ran to Ramsey via St John's and Kirk Michael.

The cars are heading to Ramsey and are not in normal service. 'Car 3' was a special, laid on for the photographic event. 2 November 2013

On the day of the photographic event some of the less common trailers were used on the normal service which added interest to the day's activities. Having just passed Ballaglass heading for Ramsey are tunnel car 9, with its lights switched on in the gloom, and one of the original 1893 lightweight trailers.

Discretion is obviously better than valour, as despite the opportunity to ride on trailer 51 in November, the absence of side shutters and the inclement weather has meant that all passengers are staying warm and dry inside the tunnel car. 2 November 2013

Returning from Ramsey is the photographers' special with 'car 3' – it is really car 2 (see previous page) – with royal trailer 59. The cars have just descended from the shoulder of the hill and are about to take the sharp left-hand turn past the Cornaa stop (pole 688) and climb away to Ballaglass.

'Cornaa', pronounced 'cornay', is another form of Corrany, which is the name of the nearby village, and both mean 'mill' or 'millstone valley'. There has been a mill at Cornaa for at least 500 years and is mentioned in 1513 in the first rent roll of the island as being owned by John McChristen (McChristian). For much of its working life the mill was owned by John's descendants, although for the last hundred years of production, it was owned by the Gelling family. It went out of use in 1951 and is now a dwelling. At one time the building included a lot of iron in its construction – lintels, joists, etc. – presumably as a fire precaution. The mill lies downhill from the tramway almost at the lower end of Ballaglass Glen. 2 November 2013

At Cornaa halt the tramway swings round a very tight curve and switches from descent to ascent; it is one of the most abrupt corners on the tramway. Beyond Cornaa the 'northbound' line actually heads south east as it skirts around the end of the Barrule range of hills in a wide loop towards Maughold.

In this view winter saloon 21 with trailer 43 are passing the stop on their way to Douglas. Note that the higher reaches of North Barrule are covered in low-lying cloud. 22 May 2009

The lower reaches of Cornaa valley are the rather unlikely venue for a factory making high explosive. In 1890 a Swedish company owned by chemist Carl Lamm started to build a factory to make Bellite, a new form of explosive which Lamm had invented. Understandably the local populace were unhappy, particularly as Lamm had been refused permission to build a plant in the UK because of safety concerns. Public outcry caused the building to be abandoned in 1892 but its concrete shell – a radical new building material in those days – may still be seen.

Tunnel car 9 and 1893 trailer 51 were last seen heading towards Ramsey at Ballaglass (see page 101). Here the weather has eased and the pair are seen returning to Douglas with a normal service. The trailer, with its minimal weather protection, is however still empty! 2 November 2013

Whilst working the last southbound service of the day tunnel car 6's lifeguard touched the track on the corner at Cornaa and was distorted enough to foul the wheels. Edwardian picturesqueness is all very well, but an eighteen mile run through often bleak countryside means that the ability to communicate with each other, the stations and the Derby Castle depot in Douglas, is, if not essential, at least extremely useful. At that time all the cars carried radio telephones – today it is more likely to be a mobile phone – and the handset is visible on the front step.

Help was therefore able to arrive fairly promptly. In the background the van can be seen parked on the northbound track in front of the shelter while the crew and the emergency response team are examining the leading truck of the car. The damaged lifeguard was removed and car 6 eventually proceeded back to Douglas arriving late and without its lifeguard. Fortunately no major damage was done to the tram and it was soon repaired. 10 May 1998

CROWCREEN

Crowcreen (pole 699) is about halfway up the climb from Cornaa on the shoulder of the hill. The name is nothing to do with the bird but derives from the Manx *creen* meaning ripe or withered and *crouw* a spreading tree growing on a single trunk, particularly one which is not very tall. Because they were ready sources of fuel, trees were relatively scarce on the Isle of Man until recently, so a spreading tree would have been very noticeable. It begs the question of why this tree was spared? There are a number of superstitions regarding the pagan sanctity of trees and this may be why the Crowcreen tree was protected.

From the slopes of North Barrule, the Isle of Man's second highest mountain and the one which dominates the north of the island, the photographer has captured winter saloon 20 and trailer 44 passing the stop heading uphill for Ramsey. In the distance the traction poles of the MER can be seen silhouetted against the Irish Sea as the line swings round the shoulder of the hill, towards Ballafayle and Ramsey. The house on the left, above the stop, has since been demolished and replaced by a largely subterranean 'eco-house' where it may sometimes be possible to see the owner mowing the roof! 6 May 2007

An intensive fifteen-minute headway service is operating as The Manx Heritage Transport Festival is under way today. There is usually a four- or five-day event like this every summer when special efforts are made to provide interesting and unusual car workings. Climbing up from Cornaa is 1893 car 2 with royal trailer 59 in tow. When driving the winter saloons the motormen are able to sit, but the older cars, including this one, require the driver to stand. With the increase in average height of population, some drivers have to stoop to see under the roof canopy.

Today car 2 reveals its true identity, unlike the photographs taken later in the year at Ballaglass and Cornaa where the tram was posing as the long-lost car 3 (see pages 101 and 102). 28 July 2013

From the eighteenth century this quarterland has been associated with the Murray family and John Murray farmed at Crowcreen in the late nineteenth century. The road crossing the tramlines is called Murray's Road, and the Crowcreen stop also uses Murray's Road as an alternative name. The 'Road' suffix was popular on UK railways, usually indicating that this was about the nearest that the railway actually got to an intended destination, which could, however, be many miles away.

Here the photographer is looking towards North Barrule which looms impressively over the Cornaa Valley. In the foreground winter saloon 22 and trailer 44 are heading towards Douglas with a 'southbound' service. Due to the loop in the line the direction that they are travelling in is actually north-west. At Cornaa, at the bottom of the hill, the line bends sharply to the south and can just be distinguished heading to the left directly above the trailer's clerestory roof. From Crowcreen it is possible to watch the cars across the valley, between Ballaglass and Cornaa. 15 September 2006

Departing from Crowcreen northbound are winter saloon 22 and trailer 41. This part of the Isle of Man is formed largely of a type of Manx slate known as Agneash grits. As such, the surface rock withstands wear and is impervious to water. Such a stable surface is an ideal platform over which to run the tramway.

The route of the track can be easily traced by the march of the traction poles into the distance. 17 May 2009

Ballaskeig (pole 718) lies at the top of the climb from Cornaa and is the first of another sequence of stops which are named after and serve farms, this time alongside the A15 road. The A15 has left the main Douglas to Ramsey road at The Hibernian and leads to the village of Maughold; the road is just off to the right of the picture. Although the 'A' prefix makes it sound like a major trunk road, in many places it is single track with passing places.

Here we see car 9 at Ballaskeig. The car has just completed the first half of a return driver experience trip (beginner's) from Ramsey and is about to cross from the southbound to the northbound line on the crossover here. The car carries illuminated boards advertising the Steam 125 event held in 1998. 14 October 1998

The derivation of the name Ballaskeig is in some doubt. The *balla* is obviously 'farm', but the skeig could either come from *skeaig*, being the Manx for hawthorn hedge, or *skeig*, from the Norse for a creek suitable for ships. Either could be appropriate, as this is a coastal stretch of the line, and more open than some of the inland parts of the route, with fewer trees and field boundaries. Two farms are served here: Ballaskeig Mooar on the seaward side of the line and Ballaskeig Beg on the landward. *Mooar* and *beg* are big and little respectively.

Fifteen years after the previous photograph was taken car 9 looks very different. Heading south with trailer 44 during the Manx Heritage Transport Festival the car approaches the access road to Ballaskeig Mooar. The A15 road runs alongside the tramway, on the far side of the track for about half a mile here and is just behind the grassy bank seen on the left. 28 July 2013

In 2008 Ballaskeig became famous during the latter part of the summer season. This was the year that considerable permanent way renewals took place and for the first part of the summer season there were no services between Laxey and Ramsey. In the second part of the season a single line of tramway was re-opened throughout and a modified service instituted. Ballaskeig was where a temporary passing loop was installed and trams from Laxey and Ramsey exchanged their single line staffs here. The first car to arrive had of necessity to await the arrival of the second but the arrangement allowed at least a restricted service. Reinstatement of both tracks over the whole length between Laxey and Ramsey meant that Ballaskeig saw far fewer cars stopping in subsequent years.

Here we see winter saloon 20 and trailer 46 approaching with a northbound service. The A15 road is beyond the bank on the right of the photograph. 14 May 2012

Heading uphill to Ramsey, blue and white liveried car 7 is running single motor. Earlier in the day car 7 had been forced to leave matching blue and white trailer 48 at Ramsey as the coupling bar had broken. A return trip to Douglas secured a replacement and trailer 48 was duly rescued and re-united with its workmate.

Here we see car 7, running solo, returning to Ramsey to collect the trailer that had been left behind earlier in the day. The intensive fifteen-minute headway service is operating, so hopefully the loss of the trailer's capacity will not be noticed too much.

The crossover seen behind car 7 was removed during the winter closure of 2013-4, although the wiring still remained *in situ*. In the distance can be seen the range of hills which stretches to Snaefell. 28 July 2013

Ballafayle Corteen (pole 731) also lies adjacent to the A15 road to Maughold. Balla is obviously 'farm' but *fayle* appears to derive from a proper name, although experts can find no trace of a Fayle family anywhere in Maughold. A similar-sounding word, *faal* is the Manx for a boundary hedge which would link with the *skeaig* of the previous stop (see page 107). At the same time *faill*, which also sounds similar, is the Manx for 'to hire', and the farm was inhabited by tenant farmers in the sixteenth century and earlier. Corteen is easier. It's a purely Manx name and is particularly connected with Maughold, especially before the nineteenth century. The family appears all over Maughold and particularly in farms in the north.

This area was the site of a serious wartime flying accident. On 8 October 1941 fifteen Hawker Hurricanes were *en route* from Fowlmere near Cambridge, England to Eglington, Derry, Northern Ireland. They were to refuel at the wartime airfields at Andreas and Jurby. Four of the Hurricanes, disorientated by low cloud, missed the aerodrome. Searching for the landing site one crashed into Snaefell and the other three into the stretch of farmland which makes up the Ballaskeigs and Ballafayles. There were no survivors. A memorial to the American pilots exists in Maughold churchyard; they were all volunteers as the US had not yet entered the war.

Here we see the last tram of the day, winter saloon 21, passing the stop and heading towards Ramsey. 5 October 2013

Looking through the back window from a passing northbound service car this 'grab' shot shows the permanent way team in action at Ballacannell (pole 733). Ballast has been collected from Dhoon Quarry, and car 7 is providing the motive power for the ballast hopper.

The southbound track has recently been relaid and ballast is being spread from the hopper wagon. Comparison of the hopper configuration with the view taken at Dhoon Quarry (see page 82) shows that the hopper size was increased after this picture was taken. The nearest crossover is at Ballaskeig, about a quarter of a mile away, so car 7 will be able to shunt clear of the southbound line to leave the way clear for the next service car to pass. 8 May 2001

Ballacannell is 'Cannell's farm' and lies only two poles away from Ballafayle Corteen. The name appears to be a contraction of Ballafyle y Cannell and there is some evidence that the farm used to be called this.

Here we see winter saloon 22 heading towards Douglas with the last afternoon departure from Ramsey. 5 October 2013

BALLAFAYLE KERRUISH

The final Ballafayle halt is Ballafayle Kerruish at pole 745. The Kerruish family is an eminent one on the island and particularly so in Maughold. Probably its most famous member was Sir Henry Charles Kerruish, the youngest and then the longest serving Speaker of the House of Keys (1962-1990). His work for increased Manx independence was tireless and he took a huge interest in the culture and heritage of his homeland. The MER has much to thank Sir Charles for as he championed

the retention of the line between Laxey and Ramsey which led to the triumphant re-opening of this section on 25 June 1977. Sir Charles cut the tape at Laxey as the first tram set off for Ramsey. Apart from the unfortunate events of 2008, when a temporary closure was in place for urgent repair work, the Laxey to Ramsey line has since operated as an integral part of the system.

A northbound service car (possibly car 20) has been halted at the stop by a flock of southbound sheep. Fortunately they don't want to board. 10 May 2000 *(Sara Goodwins)*

Ballafayle or sometimes Balyfayle is the name of the treen. Treens were typically divided into quarterlands, each quarterland forming one farm. Along this section of line, therefore, the naming of the four halts still clearly demonstrates the division of Manx land made centuries earlier. Ballafayle y Callow no longer has its own stop but would complete the quartet of Corteen, Cannell, Callow and Kerruish.

Here we see tunnel car 6 and trailer 41 with a southbound service make a longer than usual pause at the stop. The crew rounded up a sheep which had strayed onto the line and alerted the farmer. The field to the right is often home to Clydesdale and Shire horses bred here for use on the Douglas Horse Tramway and for other agricultural work. 16 May 2012

Rome's Crossing (pole 752) is one of the halts which takes its name from a person rather than a farm. The Rome family lived at Quine's Court in Ramsey, but this crossing was named after Francis Rome who lived near here in 1916. Born around 1865 he was a noted Manx Rechabite and held the office of Juvenile District Secretary.

The Independent Order of Rechabites was founded in England in 1835 as part of a wider temperance movement. A friendly society it promoted teetotalism and was named after the Old Testament Rechabites who were forbidden to drink alcohol and were forced to live a nomadic life. For this reason the different branches were known as 'Tents'.

Taken from Port Mooar, below Maughold Head, this is a long shot of winter saloon 20 with trailer 41 nearing the stop with a service for Douglas. Directly above the car, on the skyline, can be seen the stand of trees by a Quaker burial ground. In the seventeenth century most Manx members of the Society of Friends, better known as Quakers, lived in Maughold, with William Callow as their leader. Callow donated land from his farm as a burial ground for them and is himself buried there under the inscription 'William Callow of Ballafayle 1629-1676'. 18 August 2013

The Rome's Crossing halt is accessed from a lane down from the A15 road and is adjacent to the Croit Rance Holiday Cottage; Croit Rance means 'Rance's croft'.

Heading towards Ramsey we see a northbound service with blue and white liveried car 7 and trailer 48 approaching the stop. 4 August 2013

The Ballajora stop (pole 762) is situated by the level crossing where the A15 road to Maughold makes a steep descent from above the tramway into the valley. Ballajora is usually taken to mean 'the farm of the stranger', from the Manx *jiaree* or *joaree* meaning stranger. There is a suggestion that the farm was occupied by someone who had responsibilty for keeping an eye on visitors to the area, possibly some form of ecclesiastical steward. In the early mediaeval period Ballajora was owned by the Priory of St Bees. In 1175, Godred, King of Mann and the Isles, persuaded St Bees to exchange land at Dhoon and Ballelin for land in Maughold which included Ballajora.

This is the closest stop to Maughold village, famous for its church with its collection of Celtic crosses. Maughold lighthouse is beyond the village and clearly visible from a northbound tram even from as far away as Bulgham (see page 75). It is situated half-way down the cliff so that its light will show beneath the low cloud which often occurs in this area.

Here we see winter saloon 20, with dash vinyls celebrating 120 years of the MER, and trailer 46 passing the stop with a service for Ramsey. The display panel covers the large car number applied to the dash but incorporates the car number in (much) smaller characters. 4 August 2013

The side window of the shelter gives a good view of the line to the south, so that Ramsey-bound passengers can wait out of the rain yet still have time to emerge and give a clear signal to the motorman.

Still visible on Ballajora Hill (see next page), just up from the tram station, is a roadside kiln used for burning lime to provide dressing for the soil. So valuable was lime that, in 1775, Elizabeth Kermode left her husband John 'some limestones they had', and 'a feather bed for life'…! 7 May 1999 *(Sara Goodwins)*

Next to the well-maintained passenger shelter, the Victorian post box in its stone pillar is conveniently located on the corner of Ballajora Hill. The box is typical of those along the line, being installed when the tramway was extended to Ramsey in 1898, close to the end of Victorian era. The old queen died in 1901, a mere three years later. It is the only one of the original Victorian lineside post boxes to remain between Laxey and Ramsey. The post is now collected by van instead of by the MER conductors.

At the top of the hill the old chapel has been converted into a private dwelling. Ballajora Farm lies to the right of the chapel and gives its name to the area. 16 May 2012

In the foreground is pole 763. This is one of a number of poles that the MER acquired second-hand from the Southern Electric Tramway later known as the Douglas Head Marine Drive Tramway. This line had opened in 1896 and ran from the top of Douglas Head to near Port Soderic south of Douglas. Only ever a seasonal operation, it closed for business shortly after the outbreak of the Second World War in 1939. Sadly it failed to reopen after the war.

Fortunately these poles, with their distinctive collars, were not sent for scrap when the line was demolished in the post-war period They are clearly very robust and despite their age they show little sign of corrosion. They may be found at many locations along the MER and have proved to be a very economical purchase. 4 August 2013

Winter saloon 22 and an unidentified trailer are crossing Ballajora Hill and drawing to a halt opposite the shelter, having passed the former Douglas Head Marine Drive traction pole with its 'whistle' injunction.

The year 2000 saw a change in direction for the MER with the appointment of a new Director of Public Transport. The early season service was increased compared with the previous year to require three car sets, rather than two, with a more frequent service. Another initiative was the introduction of the bus style livery on car 22 – which is here looking in need of attention – during its repaint during the winter 2000-1 (see pages 8 and 73). 12 May 2000

Between Ballajora and Dreemskerry (pole 780), and nearer the latter, the remains of the workings of the Ballajora Quarry can be made out. It was served by the tramway and there was once a siding with a loading dock for stone there. At the time of writing there is still a single, severely corroded traction pole there, bereft of overhead line and some distance from the running lines. Buried in ivy are the remains of the 2'-0" gauge tramway which fed stone into the loading dock. Above the Road of Scarffe's Ridge – *Bayr Dreeyn Skerry* in Manx – which runs parallel with the tramway but further up the hill, is a second quarry, Dreemskerry Quarry. In 1961, what is now the Department of Environment, Food and Agriculture planted three hectares of largely mixed woodland in the area.

Here we see tunnel car 6 crossing Dreemskerry Hill with an unidentified trailer. Behind the station nameboard the woodland fills the hillside between the tramway and the road where the quarry lies almost directly inland of this point. 18 August 2013

There is some disagreement about whether Dreemskerry means 'Scarffe's Ridge' or not. *Dreem* is Manx for 'back' and is used for 'ridge', but the genitive of Scarffe usually becomes 'skerroo' as mentioned on page 31. Experts now appear to think that the second part of the name comes from *scarrey* meaning division or divorce. Dreemskerry seems therefore most likely to mean 'dividing ridge'. *Skerry*, a derivative of *scarrey* means 'parish' in Manx.

According to Brown's Directory of 1881, Robert Corkill was a blacksmith living and working at the Dreemskerry forge or *caardee* which may be found at the junction of Dreemskerry Hill and the Road of Scarffe's Ridge.

Here we see tunnel car 9 not in service, but being used for a tram driving experience course, approaching the stop southbound. 12 May 2000

A special service was operated on this day to commemorate 120 years of the MER, and a wide range of rolling stock was in use. Heading up the hill towards Ballajora and Douglas is the combination of 1893 car 1 and trailer 51. The conductor is at the sheltered end of the car but the motorman has no choice but to brave the elements on the open front platform. The crossover, noted in the lower caption on the page opposite, has now been removed – the nearest alternative is at Lewaigue. Points and crossings are expensive items and although crossovers provide flexibility for single-line working the cost of renewal must be justified. Accordingly the number of crossovers on the MER has reduced over the years. 7 September 2013

A few minutes later we see sister car 2, which also dates from the opening of the line, heading in the opposite direction. This time the royal trailer, 59, provides a more welcoming environment than the facilities of the open trailer attached to car 1.

Note the gartered device on the door to the platform: '120 Years of the MER' is written on the garter and below in the horizontal bar '1893-2013'. Cars 1 and 2 are the oldest tramcars in the world still in use on their original line. That they still fully operational and can appear on ordinary services indicates that the MER appreciates the value of this unique pair of vehicles. 7 September 2013

On the penultimate weekend of the 2013 season car 1, also with the 120 years garter device, has paused at Dreemskerry on its way to Ramsey. This is not a normal service car and No. 1 is running ahead of the first scheduled northbound tram. The photographer was pleased to obtain this picture as he was waiting for the first southbound service car which was due a few minutes later.

The shelter at Dreemskerry is one of the traditional corrugated iron structures and is tucked into the hillside. It is not the most attractive but includes seating and a timetable, and successfully shelters passengers from the rain – which is, after all, the point! 26 October 2013

Looking at the retreating car 9 we see that the sunlight has caught the array of light bulbs that were installed when it was first fitted with illuminations in 1993. Time has passed and the end illuminated boards bear no significant message, just white spaces.

Having completed a journey from Douglas to Ramsey the trainee motorman (see page 115) is now on the homeward leg. Two to three poles ahead of the tram it is just possible to make out the former crossover which was opposite Ballajora Quarry which was convenient for shunting stone wagons to and from the quarry sidings. 12 May 2000

DREEMSKERRY FARM

Dreemskerry Farm (pole 795) is unusual in that there is no public access to the stop other than by tram. The stop only serves the farm and there is no right of way through this private property. It is, however, permissable to alight here and join a later service.

In 1867 the farm was owned by Ewan Christian who also owned much of Lewaigue; the Christian family is one of the island's premier families. The previous buildings were cleared from the site and the current dwelling – just off the left of this picture – was completed in 2009.

This view is taken from the Maughold Brooghs. Tunnel car 6 and trailer 46 are climbing from Lewaigue and will very shortly pass the stop at Dreemskerry Farm on the long steady climb to Dreemskerry itself. 16 May 2012

Having alighted at the stop, the first passing tram to come into the photographer's viewfinder was winter saloon 21 heading for Douglas. Behind the tram the stop flag at Lewaigue can just be discerned before the tramway turns to the right.

The straight section of line between Dreemskerry and Lewaigue is the longest on the MER. 14 September 2011

Dreemskerry Farm is probably the most prominent building in the valley. The MER flag for the stop is just visible through the foliage, with Port-e-Vullen in the distance. Please note: the photograph is taken from private property. 1 July 2013 *(Sara Goodwins)*

The valley which runs south-east from Lewaigue to Port Mooar marks the course of an ancient river and is a relic of the ice age. In 1897 a proposal was passed by Tynwald for the MER to run on a low level route along the shore at Port Lewaigue. The plans would have taken the line eastwards from Dreemskerry towards Gob ny Rona across the valley and then run close to sea level rejoining the current route north of Bellevue. There are some signs of this at Port Lewaigue, principally the partly-built sea wall. The scheme was abandoned however and although the reason was never published, problems were reported with the underlying geology of the area; certainly the area floods at times of heavy rain. In addition the cliffs near Ballure are not the most stable and remedial works have been necessary in recent years.

Here we see an unusual conjunction of cars. Nearest to the photographer is winter saloon 20, which has turned its trolley pole to conduct a reversing movement. Meanwhile tunnel car 6 and trailer 41 are drawing up to face car 20. At this time work was in progress near the Ballure cliffs and single line working was in force, using the southbound line. Until the southbound service car has cleared the crossover under car 6 these cars will be held here. Having drawn forward, the tunnel car and trailer will reverse and proceed to Ramsey (the driver having been given a single line ticket) followed by car 20 with the staff. Car 20 is on a driver experience course but 6 and 41 are the service cars. 16 May 2012 *(Sara Goodwins)*

Lewaigue (pole 811) is situated at the crossing of a minor road on which is situated the Lewaigue Venture Centre – a source of many young passengers on the MER in the summer months. The derivation of the name is a little obscure but is usually accepted to mean 'creek of the slope'. It is possible that the 'lew' part of the name is an anglicised spelling of the Manx *slieau* (mountain). The Manx word *aeg* means 'young' or 'underdeveloped'. Potentially then the hill which rises to the west of Lewaigue could be a 'young' or 'small' mountain.

Interestingly Lewaigue is pronounced 'Layg' as a single syllable, as opposed to Kewaigue in Braddan, which, differing only in its first letter, is pronounced with two syllables, i.e. 'Kew-ayg'.

Beside the northbound line is this waiting shelter, a shiplap wooden building which dates from the late 1980s. 14 May 2012

Shortly after the upper photograph on page 119 was taken we see car 5 and trailer 47 passing Lewaigue southbound. Car 5 has recently been repainted and has now reverted to 'Manx Electric Railway' on the bodyside. Previously it had operated with the Manx equivalent, *Raad-Yiarn Lectragh Vannin* (see page 34). The edges of the step are highlighted in yellow and white wall tyres are visible on the wheels in this early season view. 16 May 2012

Running north on the southbound line are winter saloon 20 and trailer 46. These cars have waited at Lewaigue for a southbound car to clear the single line section and, having used the crossover, are now setting off for Ramsey. 14 May 2012

Capturing three cars on the line in one picture is very rare, particularly north of Laxey. Here we see the retreating car 5 and trailer 47 climbing up the hill to Dreemskerry. The conductor from car 6 is losing no time in changing the points for cars 6 and 41 to start their reversing manoeuvre onto the wrong line while car 20 waits patiently for the other cars to clear the way (see also page 119). Lewaigue is the first crossover south of Ramsey and in the peak season the operation of this section under single line rules can be challenging: carrying out a return trip to Ramsey, including shunting the trailer and getting back to Lewaigue before the next northbound car arrives can be a little tight. Pole number 811 leaves us with no doubt as to the location. Incidentally, the cross above the number on car 20 is not something odd inside the motorman's cab, but is a reflection in the window of the level crossing sign for motorists on the road which crosses the tracks where the photographer is standing. 16 May 2012 *(Sara Goodwins)*

Bellevue (pole 840) is named after a large house in the area, which is now known as Faaie Mooar, or sometimes Faaie Mooar Folieu. In Manx *faaie mooar folieu* means 'a large well-manured field near a manor house under a mountain' (the derivation of Fairy Cottage may have similar roots – see page 39). Built in the Georgian style in 1828 by Mr G Stephen, Faaie Mooar is noted for its beautiful and ornamental gardens which cover more than six acres. In 1883 the house was occupied by Mr Thomas Allen, possibly from the same family who gave their name to Ballelin (see page 85). Today Faaie Mooar is occasionally used by the Isle of Man film industry.

Bellevue, in common with Glen Mona, used to have a postbox but this has now been removed; the photographer is standing close to its former location. The wooden shelter is relatively recent. Following a campaign by local residents the planned green steel and glass bus shelter was not erected here. Approaching with a southbound service are winter saloon 21 and trailer 43. 20 May 2009

Unusually the station nameboard is not placed on top of the waiting shelter, but situated opposite above a fence painted in MER green. Port-e-Vullen is a village on the coast, and is reached by following the road down the hill from the stop. The old spelling was Purt y Wyllin or Port ny Mwyllin, meaning 'Harbour of the Mill'. The mill in question was Lewaigue mill and no longer exists; the last miller to work there emigrated to the USA in 1840. The dwelling, 'The Anchorage', now occupies the site. 27 September 2013

The road which crosses the tramway at Bellevue is the A15 which loops through Maughold to Ramsey. Looking down the steep drop from near where the A15 leaves the A2 we see that winter saloon 19 and trailer 48 have just left Bellevue with a southbound service over the oblique crossing.

Beyond the tram can be seen two substantial gateposts: the name reads 'Faaie Moar' and leads to the house mentioned in the caption on the previous page. Due to the length of the lens used for this photograph, the gate posts are actually substantially further from the tramway than they appear. 9 May 2007

Between Bellevue and the next stop, Ballure, the line runs close to the clifftop. The cliffs have been a cause of concern in recent years and remedial works to protect them from erosion and to strengthen the upper sections have been carried out. The contractor's need for access resulted in single-line working on the MER. Early in 2012 the northbound line, i.e. the line furthest from the sea, was closed. Then during 2013 it was the turn of the seaward-side line to be closed for parts of the season. Single-line working operated between Ramsey and Lewaigue.

In this view car 9 and trailer 46 are departing from Bellevue with a northbound service on the wrong line. Extra care is needed by the motorman at level crossings with restricted sight lines such as at Bellevue, as road users will not be expecting the trams to appear on the wrong side of the tracks. It is one of the many occasions where the tram's whistle comes into its own. 16 May 2012

Also crossing the road at Bellevue we see tunnel car 6 with trailer 46 heading towards Douglas; the combination clearly illustrates the abrupt change in the gradient at this point.

On the right, partially hidden by the road sign is the electrical substation which transforms high tension AC power taken directly from the grid, into low voltage DC power which is fed to the overhead. There is an electric feeder point at the first pole beyond the crossing, so the motorman will need to coast past the pole. The substation was introduced in 1934 as part of the modernization of the power supply system when the power station at Ballaglass was decommissioned. 2 May 2004

The Lewaigue Venture Centre, situated up the hill from Lewaigue tramstop and previousy part of a large farm, was founded in 1981 and has been run since then by the Read family. Its groups of excited youngsters generate a significant proportion of the traffic to and from the Lewaigue stop. Here winter saloon 20 is hauling trailer 47 which is almost filled to capacity by a group from the centre on their way to some outdoor adventure. The trailer is crossing the road at Bellevue and the station nameboard on the right of the picture is framed by the verticals of the trailer body. And, yes, that was a fluke! 19 May 2010

Looking from the crossing with the footpath, Ballure Walk, winter saloon 22 and trailer 44 form a southbound service. At Ballure (pole 869) the tramway finally reconnects with the Douglas to Ramsey main road, last seen near Glen Mona (see page 90). The crossing is one of only three on the MER which are protected by lights.

The car set has crossed the main road and cleared the traffic lights, allowing the waiting silver car to cross. The traffic lights are triggered, and cleared, by treadles in the track: a white light indicates to the motorman that road traffic has the flashing red lights and he should be able to proceed safely. The viaduct has a speed limit of 5 mph. In practice this means first notch on the controller as the cars are not equipped with speedometers.

On the viaduct the permanent way features extra check rails to the outside of the running rails. In the event of a derailment these should prevent the tramcar's wheels straying too far from their intended course and prevent the tram falling into the Ballure River below.

The decking of the viaduct is not solid and from an open trailer the handrail beside the track is also well below reach so there is a feeling of being suspended above nothing. Naturally pedestrians are not permitted to walk along the viaduct, so the only view of the drop is from the tram. 11 May 2007

Ballure is derived from *balley euar* meaning 'yew tree farm'. Ballure Cottage is on the right of the line, probably built around the end of the eighteenth century and occupied by the Christian family. In the garden is a huge ancient yew tree. Yews live a very long time so this tree might be the one which gave Ballure its name.

Immediately south of the stop and the road crossing is the Ballure Viaduct, the only structure of its kind on the MER. Initially the Ramsey extension was delayed by the effort required to span the river gorge here, and a temporary terminus operated on the south side of the chasm from 2 August 1898. The line was

finally opened through to Ramsey across the new steel viaduct on 24 July 1899. Here we are looking at the rear of tunnel car 6 and trailer 46 as they cross the viaduct and approach the road crossing. 9 May 2007

Work is in progress on the northbound line just to the south of the Ballure Viaduct. The work site is duly fenced off from the southbound line and there is no access from the Ballure Walk. Remedial work has taken place to contain the landside embankment following which new track and ballast has been laid. The overhead line has been removed over this track – as can be seen from the absence of the support arms – so that engineering plant cannot accidentally come into contact with live wires.

Today is Monday; by the end of the week the overhead will be reinstated and the single line working will have come to an end. Car 6 proceeds on the southbound line and the photograph is taken from trailer 47. 14 May 2012

The geological problems with the Ballure Cliffs and the remedial works required single line working in both 2012 and 2013. When running wrong line the first treadle to be reached would normally clear the traffic signals and the second would set them. Additional push buttons are placed for the crew's use when running wrong line so that the signals are set manually before arrival and also cleared manually after crossing the road.

Here a northbound service on the southbound line has paused to allow the conductor to press the button to reset the traffic lights. Car 5 and trailer 47 will now continue into Ramsey. 15 May 2012

When technology fails the crew revert to older procedures. Despite pressing the button the lights have not come on so the conductor has got down to walk in front of the car and stand in the road with the red flag to stop the traffic and allow car 6 and 41 to proceed safely. The conductor will then reboard at the rear platform on another wrong-line service to Ramsey. The red flag is an essential piece of tramway and railway safety equipment carried by all conductors and guards. 16 May 2012

For much of 2013 the seaward-side line was closed and all services used the northbound line. Here we see car 5 and trailer 47 passing the stop under the protection of the traffic signals and heading, wrong line, towards Douglas. The car will pause in about a hundred yards time for the motorman to press the button to clear the road signals.

The photographer is standing where the line crosses Ballure Walk. The footpath has left the main road on the south side of the valley at Lhergy Frissel ('Frissel's hill'), at the top of which is the Albert Tower. Ballure Walk leads down into the valley, crosses the stream and emerges through stone arches onto the beach. The Frissel of Lhergy Frissel is John Frissel, Attorney General and MHK. His son John was the first High Bailiff of Ramsey. 27 September 2013

During the 2013 peak summer period, normal service was operated over both lines, as can be seen from the shiny top surface of the rails. Looking from the minor road which runs close to the line north of Ballure, winter saloon 21 and trailer 41 have crossed the viaduct and are about to cross the main road with a northbound service.

To the left of the line in the background we can see that work continues behind the fence on the edge of the cliff. In the shoulder season single-line working was reintroduced, as seen in the previous photograph. 11 August 2013

Queen's Valley stop (pole 880) was created in 2007 to serve the new housing estate of the same name that was completed in 2008. Ironically the closure of the Laxey to Ramsey section for much of the 2008 season meant that the stop saw little service in its first year.

From Ballure the line passes through the outskirts of Ramsey behind back gardens and across suburban roads. Ballure Chapel, now a private dwelling, overlooks Queen's valley from the north and is believed to have been dedicated to St Catherine. It was probably one of the original keeills in the area, which means the foundations were built around 1200. From 1600-1822, when St Paul's was built in Ramsey, Ballure Chapel was used as a chapel of ease for Kirk Maughold – Ramsey was growing fast but had no church of its own. Extended in 1745 the chapel was disused from the 1980s and sold into private ownership in 2005 when it was converted to a dwelling.

Here we see winter saloon 19 with trailer 41 approaching from Ramsey. Behind the car can be seen the houses in Walpole Road: the next stop is a few poles away by tram, but a much longer walk by road. 22 May 2009

Descending from Ballure, winter saloon 19 is approaching Queen's Valley with a service for Ramsey. After two years additional wear the paint finish is showing definite signs of deterioration compared with the photograph above. Winter saloons typically need the bodywork refurbishing about every five years. The gardens of the new estate are to the right of the photograph.

The stop is where the road crosses into Ballure Grove and is, at the time of writing, the only road crossing on the MER without yellow hatching painted on its surface. This is slightly ironic as, from the east, the tarmaced road is below the level of the tramway and the crossing is not easy to spot if drivers miss the signage. 11 September 2011

Walpole Drive (pole 885) marks the point where the MER joins Walpole Road. Many British politicians come from the Walpole family, but the most important from the Isle of Man's point of view was Spencer Walpole, who was Lieutenant Governor of the island from 1882 to 1893. He was particularly noted for his financial acumen.

Ramsey's Queen's Pier was completed during Walpole's time in office and, as the land at this end of town was developed, Walpole Road (alongside which the tramway runs) and Walpole Drive were both named after the governor. Car 5 and trailer 44 are descending from the Queen's Valley stop towards Ramsey. 11 August 2013

When the line was laid alongside Walpole Road it had been the intention that the road would be paved. Accordingly the line from this stop to Queen's Drive, unlike most of the rest of the track, was laid with grooved tram rails, while the overhead was supported from side bracket arms, rather than having centre poles. The original rails were replaced with standard flat bottom rails in due course but this section still retains the traction poles on the landward side with both lines of overhead cantilevered across the tracks. Evidently the paving has yet to be installed.

The new tracks laid in Laxey Station during the 2013-14 winter closure saw a more recent use of grooved tramway rail on the MER, and also on the Snaefell Mountain Railway. 22 May 2009

Winter saloon 21 and trailer 47 have climbed up from the Queen's Drive stop. Examination of the track shows that this section was relaid between the date of this photograph and the one from 2009 above.

The Isle of Man Transport lettering is looking the worse for wear on the dash. This style was applied to the bus fleet but has now been superseded by the 'Bus Vannin' branding and no longer adorns the tramcars. 8 May 2005

Queen's Drive (pole 890) is the nearest stop to the Isle of Man's sole surviving iron pier which was opened on 22 July 1886 and allowed to be christened 'Queen's Pier' by gracious permission of Queen Victoria. At the time, Ramsey was being developed to provide lodging houses for visitors as well as dwellings for the more well-to-do residents. By a natural association of ideas the road leading to Queen's Pier became Queen's Drive.

From the Queen's Drive end of Walpole Road winter saloon 19 and trailer 41 draw away on the final part of their journey to Ramsey. Unusually the stop flag is attached to a lampost in Queen's Drive, rather than being fixed to the nearest traction pole. 22 May 2009

Looking back along Walpole Road winter saloon 21 and trailer 47 are also heading towards Ramsey, and approaching the junction with Queen's Drive. The high hedge – which is in someone's garden and therefore not removable by the MER – means that the sightlines here are extremely poor and motormen approach with extra caution. There are a number of driveways which cross the tracks and lead onto the road which require those living in the houses to show tolerance to their tramway neighbours. 10 September 2006

Ballastowell (pole 898) lies just outside Ramsey Station. Clearly the name means 'Stowell's Farm', but unusually the name can be traced to a pair of individuals. In 1511 Donald and William McStoile held a quarterland in the treen of Cardle. In 1847, at the time of the visit to Ramsey by Queen Victoria, Mr Edward Stowell, presumably a descendent of the McStoiles, lived here. The area is obviously no longer farmed being part of the town of Ramsey.

At the stop a footpath leads down from the Brogh, which is Manx for 'bank' – in the sense of a hill and not a financial institution – and crosses the line to pass between the houses of Waterloo Road.

Here tunnel car 6 and trailer 41 are heading into Ramsey. The cars are running wrong-line due to remedial works being carried out on the cliffs near Ballure. On the left of the picture can be seen the corrugated iron clad Ramsey car shed which stables a car set overnight during the operating season. 16 May 2012

As winter saloon 22 departs from Ramsey with a driver experience training car, the instructor is probably warning the trainee to be wary of the photographer who is on the footpath below the line. In the background can just be seen the trailer of the next southbound service waiting departure in Ramsey Station. On this day single-line working was in operation and the crew member in charge of car 22 will have been shown the single-line staff and then given a ticket granting him authority to use the line. The staff itself will be carried by the conductor of the service car which will follow car 22 on the single line section (see also page 119-21). 16 May 2012

What a lash up! By the footpath crossing is an unconventional piece of track, to say the least. Evidently the rails were not quite to gauge so one is being held in place by a fishplate which is spiked to the outside of the sleeper. Having demonstrated how *not* to do it, this particular item was removed and the track relaid correctly during the 2008 closure of the Laxey to Ramsey section. 7 May 2007

The final stop on the line is Ramsey and the ultimate traction pole bears the number 903. The tramway finally reached Ramsey in 1899 with services operating from 24 July. There had been an interlude of almost a year while the viaduct at Ballure was constructed and the tram tracks laid into the town. The temporary terminus on the far side of the valley at Ballure was superseded by the new station close to the town centre.

Ramsey is the second largest town on the Isle of Man and has a sheltered harbour where the Sulby River flows into the Irish Sea. The name Ramsey is generally acknowledged to mean 'wild garlic river' although there are some thoughts it could mean 'raven's water'.

The station building shown here was constructed in 1964. At the time of writing there are plans to redevelop the site as a combined bus and tram interchange station with consequent closure of the existing bus station, which is about two hundred yards away. 21 May 2009

The approach to Ramsey from the south passes the car shed on the sea side of the line and then drops down across Parsonage Road to the terminus. A single car will enter the station directly but a car with a trailer will halt just clear of the road crossing. Here tunnel car 7 with an unidentified trailer has halted to allow passengers to alight. Car 7 will draw forward and reverse over the crossover while the trailer is allowed to roll down into the station under gravity, controlled by the conductor on the hand brake. The motor car will then couple up to the Douglas end of the trailer and with a final swing of the trolley pole the car set will be left ready to board for the next journey south. Meanwhile the crew will adjourn for a well earned cup of tea in the station building. 12 May 1998

Illuminated tunnel car 9 is part way through the shunting process: car 9 has uncoupled from trailer 45, drawn forward and reversed over the crossover. The two cars are now side by side on the approaches to the station. The conductor is on board trailer 45 and is turning the hand brake wheel so that it will start the final few yards of its journey to the end of the line. Meanwhile the trolley pole has been turned and car 9 is ready shunt down and be reunited with its trailer.

Due to an anticipated high level of engineering work, trailer 45 was temporarily converted into an additional works flat car about 2004 and the bodywork removed. At the time of writing the wooden superstructure has not been replaced so more recent views of 45 do not show it as a passenger vehicle. 13 May 1998

Seen from the Parsonage Road level crossing the shunt move involving winter saloon 22 and trailer 41 is in progress. Car 22 has reversed out of the way of the trailer, but the trolley pole has not yet been swung. Trailer 41 has its handbrake on and the station master and platform crew are about to organize the safe movement of trailer 41 into the station. Until this has taken place all passengers are required to remain by the station building. Visible to the left of car 41 is The Shed which is a Ramsey-based youth club based in what was originally the Ramsey goods shed. There is still track leading to the building but it is no longer used by the tramway. 10 May 2005

Ramsey station is designed with a slight slope so that the trailers can be coasted under gravity from the Parsonage Road end to beyond the crossover. At least, that's the aim. Usually a trailer needs a bit of a push to get started. Here the motorman of car 21 gives trailer 43 a heave, while his conductor is still turning the trolley on the winter saloon. On rare occasions a recalcitrant trailer might need to be pushed the whole distance. While the trailer is moving the crewmember in charge of it – which could be the motorman, conductor, or even the Ramsey stationmaster – stands facing in the direction of travel ready to brake as required.

An earth bank is provided as a buffer at the end of the track just in case the brakes fail or the conductor misjudges the speed of the coasting car. 23 May 2009

Once the trailer is in position and braked, the motor car is reversed down to it to be re-coupled. The Hughes' patent coupling is aligned before the motor car begins to move and the conductor stands in front of the end of the trailer with the coupling bar already fitted. The driver slows the motor car, obeying hand and voice signals from the conductor and the two vehicles are brought together. Once the tow bar is engaged, it is anchored in place and the safety chain, which will activate the trailer's brakes should the tow bar fail, is attached.

The procedure sounds complicated but skill and long usage have made crews very proficient and the whole process probably takes no more than three or four minutes.

Roger Sayle, for many years the conductor on cars which started at Ramsey, and later the Ramsey stationmaster, here couples winter saloon 21 to trailer 46. 7 May 2002

While the crews work to turn the sets, passengers wait safely by the station building. There is little doubt where!

Here winter saloon 20 and trailer 41 have just arrived and are about to begin the shunting process. 8 May 1996 *(Sara Goodwins)*

The car shunting sequence is complete and the coupled cars are awaiting passengers from Ramsey. Here winter saloon 19 and trailer 48 are in matching historic livery of cream and varnished wood, with the motor car bearing the legend 'Douglas, Laxey & Ramsey Electric Tramway'; the trailer has 'Manx Electric Railway' above the footboard.

Trailer 48 has featured in at least three different liveries over the period covered by this book. As well as the one shown here, at the time of writing, it wears the blue and white livery matching car 7 (see page 74 and others) and has also appeared – although not, unfortunately in this book – in the red and white colours usually associated with the MER. 4 May 1998

During normal service hours there is usually not more than one tram at Ramsey. The time between arrival and departure is a quarter of an hour, except at the middle of the day when the crew have three-quarters of an hour for lunch. The presence of illuminated tunnel car 9 and winter saloon 22 together is because car 9 is employed on a driver experience training run and is not in normal service. Car 22 will depart first with the normal service so that the training car, which may be slower, cannot cause delays to fare-paying passengers.

The northern section of the line is often preferred for driver experience excursions as it is generally quieter and hence presents fewer hazards to (and from) inexperienced motormen. There are no trailers running at this late point in the season so no shunting either. 14 October 1998

Ramsey used to be known as Ramsey (Plaza), this being the name of the cinema located on what is now the car park. Originally the building had been opened as the Palace Concert Hall and Ballroom in the early 1890s and was purchased by the MER's predecessors in 1897, two years before the tramway arrived in town. Having been leased to various operators it was sold in 1938. Its first use as a cinema was under the name of the 'Manx Picturedrome' in 1912 and it became the Plaza on modernization. After closing as a cinema in 1974 it became a leisure centre from 1976 to 1978 finally being demolished 1990-1. The space where it used to be is now the car park visible to the left of the picture.

The original Ramsey Station was equipped with wooden kiosks as at Laxey (see page 51) and which could once have been found at Garwick Glen (see page 35) when there was an appreciable tourist trade there.

The general colour of the MER traction poles is green, but those in Ramsey Station are now painted dark red. As is visible here, they were orginally green but in 2003-4 were repainted to match the woodwork of the station building.

From inside the royal saloon winter saloon 19 can be seen moving down to collect the trailer to return it to Douglas. Originally built as the directors' saloon, the small trailer includes historic photographs mounted in the eaves and delicately etched glass in the clerestory. The royal trailer is considerably shorter than any of the other passenger cars on the MER and the reduced distance between the bogie centres gives a ride which is very different from any of the other trams with a higher frequency of oscillation – not uncomfortable or unpleasant – but not the same as the other cars. Basically, it waddles! 7 May 1998

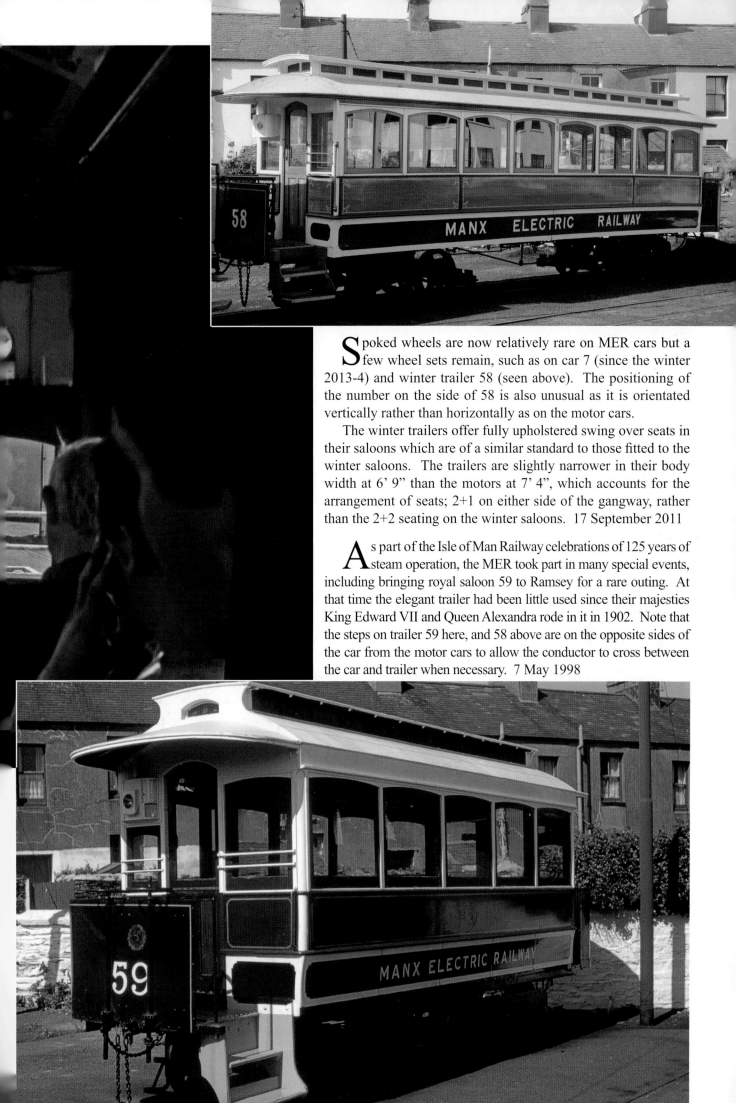

S poked wheels are now relatively rare on MER cars but a few wheel sets remain, such as on car 7 (since the winter 2013-4) and winter trailer 58 (seen above). The positioning of the number on the side of 58 is also unusual as it is orientated vertically rather than horizontally as on the motor cars.

The winter trailers offer fully upholstered swing over seats in their saloons which are of a similar standard to those fitted to the winter saloons. The trailers are slightly narrower in their body width at 6' 9" than the motors at 7' 4", which accounts for the arrangement of seats; 2+1 on either side of the gangway, rather than the 2+2 seating on the winter saloons. 17 September 2011

A s part of the Isle of Man Railway celebrations of 125 years of steam operation, the MER took part in many special events, including bringing royal saloon 59 to Ramsey for a rare outing. At that time the elegant trailer had been little used since their majesties King Edward VII and Queen Alexandra rode in it in 1902. Note that the steps on trailer 59 here, and 58 above are on the opposite sides of the car from the motor cars to allow the conductor to cross between the car and trailer when necessary. 7 May 1998

Having shunted trailer 47, backed car 20 down, coupled up and turned the trolley the crew have adjourned for a cup of tea in the station building. The car set is awaiting passengers at least one of whom prefers to sit on the bench and in the sun for the time being.

The building behind the tram opened in 2013 as the Ramsey Heritage Centre, previously having been known as Quayle's Hall and built in 1837 as a presbyterian church. Anyone returning too early for their tram might find something of interest inside. 11 May 2005

An unusual combination of cars is found waiting at Ramsey, with 1906 open motor 33 and winter trailer 57 lined up for departure. This was the 120th anniversary of the opening of the MER in 1893, so a special high-frequency service is in operation. In keeping with the spirit of the celebrations, the management has made sure that there are plenty of opportunities to ride on some of the less frequently used cars. Note: unlike car 58 (see previous page) the side number of car 57 is painted on horizontally above the windows below the roof line. 7 September 2013

From the far side of Parsonage Road blue-and-white-liveried car 7 and trailer 48 can be seen departing Ramsey for Douglas. In the grass to the right of car 7 is the headshunt of the Ramsey car shed. Overnight the shed will hold the last car (and trailer) to arrive at Ramsey which will then be used to work the first service to Douglas the following morning. The two-road shed has some storage space and lies between the tramway and Waterloo Road. It was originally erected at Ballure and moved to Ramsey when the line was extended in 1899. 14 May 2012

In reflective mood! At the crossing with Parsonage Road immediately outside Ramsey station a strategically placed mirror gives the motorman a view of traffic approaching from the side road – and vice versa. Here the mirror gives a reversed image of cars 5 and 47. 15 May 2012 *(Sara Goodwins)*

The facilities listed below are not necessarily owned or managed by the MER and are correct at the time of writing. The halts are listed in order from Douglas to Ramsey and the number in brackets refers to the pole number of the stop. Please note: if the name of a halt is omitted then it has no passenger facilities.

Derby Castle (1)	Ticket office (open), bus-type shelter, benches, pay toilets, refreshments available in Terminus Tavern
Port Jack (16)	Toilets, refreshments available in Port Jack Chippy
Onchan Head (33)	Bus-type shelter
Boncompte/Churchill (46)	Refreshments available in Majestic Chinese Restaurant
Majestic (51)	Bus-type shelter
Far End (66)	Bus-type shelter
Howstrake (88)	Concrete shelter (privately owned and now fenced off)
Groudle Old Road (107)	Bus-type shelter
Groudle Glen (117)	Ticket office (disused), large open-fronted wooden shelter, benches, post box
Baldromma/Halfway/ Liverpool Arms (179)	Bus-type shelter, post box, refreshments available in the Liverpool Arms
Baldrine (215)	Green corrugated-iron shelter with bench seating, post box
Ballagawne (257)	Bus-type shelter
Ballabeg (282)	Green corrugated-iron shelter with bench seating
Fairy Cottage (307)	Green corrugated-iron shelter with bench seating
South Cape (320)	Open-fronted green corrugated-iron shelter with bench seating
Laxey Station (359)	Ticket office (open), waiting room, benches, toilets, post box, refreshments available in station café and Mines Tavern
Dumbell's Row (372)	Bus-type shelter, refreshments available in 'Laxey's' (formerly Brown's Café), off-road parking
Minorca (409)	Green corrugated-iron shelter with bench seating
Bulgham (507)	Platform
Dhoon Glen (531)	Wooden shelter with bench, chairs, toilets, refreshments available in Dhoon Glen café (note: open seasonally), off-road parking
Glen Mona (611)	Wooden shelter with bench seating
Ballaglass (654)	Wooden shelter with gate and bench seating
Cornaa (688)	Green wooden shelter with bench seating
Ballaskeig (718)	Green corrugated-iron shelter (privately provided), small and extremely overgrown
Rome's crossing (752)	Covered bench seat (privately provided)
Ballajora (762)	Green corrugated-iron shelter with bench seating, post box
Dreemskerry (780)	Green corrugated-iron shelter with bench seating
Dreemskerry Farm (795)	Covered bench seat (privately provided)
Lewaigue (811)	Wooden shelter with bench seating
Bellevue (840)	Open-fronted wooden shelter with bench seating
Ramsey (903)	Ticket office (open), waiting room, benches, toilets, car park

SELECTED BIBLIOGRAPHY

Basnett, Stan, *Trams of the Isle of Man 1946-Present Day*, Lily Publications, Undated c.2008

Broderick, George, *A Dictionary of Manx Place Names*, English Place Name Society, 2006

Edwards, Barry, *The Manx Electric Railway*, B&C Publications, 1998

Edwards, Barry, *The Railways and Tramways of the Isle of Man*, Oxford Publishing Co., 1993

Edwards, Barry, *Trains and Trams of the Isle of Man*, Lily Publications, 2010

Goodwyn, Mike, *All about the Manx Electric Railway*, Manx Electric Railway Society, 1989

Goodwyn, Mike, *Douglas Head Marine Drive and Electric Tramway*, Manx Electric Railway Society, 1978

Goodwyn, Mike, *Manx Electric*, Platform 5 Publishing Ltd., 1993

Heavyside, Tom, *Douglas – Laxey – Ramsey*, Middleton Press, 2010

Hendry, Robert, *Rails in the Isle of Man*, Midland Publishing, 1993

Hendry, Robert P., *Manx Electric Railway Saga*, Adam Gordon, 2010

Hendry, Dr. R Preston and Hendry, R. Powell, *Manx Electric Railway Album*, Hillside Publishing Co., 1978

Jones, Norman, *Isle of Man Tramways*, Foxline Publishing, Undated c. 1993

Kneen, J.J., *The Place-Names of the Isle of Man, Part III – Sheading of Garff*, Yn Cheshaght Ghailckagh, 1926

Kniveton, Gordon N., *The Onchan Story*, The Manx Experience, 1992

Moore, A.W., *The Surnames & Place Names of the Isle of Man*, Elliot Stock, 1890

Pearson, F.K., *Isle of Man Tramways*, David & Charles, 1970

Pearson, Keith, *One Hundred Years of the Manx Electric Railway*, Leading Edge Press and Publishing, 1992

Quilliam, Leslie, *A Gazetteer of the Isle of Man*, Cashtal Books, 2004

Radcliffe, William and Constance, *Maughold and Ramsey Place-names*, Radcliffe, 1978

Periodicals

Manx Transport Review, occasionally, various issues, Manx Electric Railway Society
Trams Magazine, quarterly, various issues, Train Crazy Publishing